Praise for

Graham was one of the best I've seen at asking for referrals. *Just Ask!* is a testament to his excellent work. I recommend this book to any business that wants to grow by asking for referrals.

Tucker York
Goldman Sachs: Global Co-head of Consumer
and Wealth Management

Just Ask! is an apt and appropriate title. This is a book that all salespeople should own. If you want more high-quality clients, try asking for referrals. This excellent guide will show you how.

Brett Lankester
Former CEO, London, Union Bancaire Privee

As Graham says 'Referrals are a hidden gem' and here are the tips, techniques and strategies for you to get more business. An excellent book.

Philip Hesketh
Best Selling Author, *Persuade*
World Authority on Influence and Persuasion

This is an excellent book on an important topic, and I highly recommend it for entrepreneurs, sales executives, and others interested in building a business

Philip Anderson
Insead: Professor of Entrepreneurship

I wish I'd had this book 20 years ago! Relationships have always been at the heart of my psychology business; but asking for referrals has never been. *Just Ask!* is one of those rare books that highlights a gap that is bleeding obvious after you've read it. You will find yourself thinking 'So true' frequently, but right at the point when you start beating yourself up, *Just Ask!* gently and clearly builds your confidence and excitement to start asking.

Tony Crabbe
International Best Selling Author, *Busy*
Business Psychologist

Praise for Graham Eisner

Graham has helped advisers get over the natural mindset block that typically impedes asking for a referral. I would recommend Graham to any organization.

Rory Dorman
Head of Sales
MASECO Private Wealth

The techniques learnt are now being actively applied by the team out in the field. I cannot recommend this session highly enough.

Nick Heath
Head of Business Development
Seven Investment Management

I cannot recommend this book highly enough. By following Graham's powerful approach and methodology, my team successfully re-engineered its approach to interacting with clients. Applying these ideas and principles has led to increased referral levels whilst deepening our client relationships.

Mark Entwistle
Compass Rose Investments

We are progressing well in regard to referrals applying some of the frameworks Graham took us through and have achieved a 20% increase in volume in the last quarter alone.

Dan Archer
Marketing Director
383 Digital Studios

JUST ASK!

7 simple steps to unlock the power of clients, **generate referrals** and **double your business**

GRAHAM EISNER

First published in Great Britain by Practical Inspiration Publishing, 2022

ISBN   978-1-78860-321-8 (print)
          978-1-78860-319-5 (epub)
          978-1-78860-320-1 (mobi)

Practical Inspiration
Publishing

MIX
Paper from
responsible sources
FSC   www.fsc.org   FSC® C171272

To my parents, who gave me the mixture of personality characteristics that have helped me in my career at Goldman Sachs and as a sales coach and trainer.

Contents

Foreword

'If you don't ask, you don't get' was the oft-repeated refrain of my first boss in the financial services industry. And yet, despite this constant reminder, asking was significantly more difficult than I could possibly imagine. Asking for a mandate, asking for a referral, it seemed intrusive, occasionally unseemly and as with all naked questions, the fear of rejection was tangible. Within our midst, however, was one individual with a clear knowledge and understanding – not only of the benefit of successfully asking difficult questions, but also how to do it. Graham Eisner was that individual and throughout his successful career at Goldman Sachs, was, in consequence, the outstanding new business winner of his generation.

The 'how' is key. In this excellent book Graham explains with remarkable simplicity his approach to generating business via referrals, leading to the growth of one's client base. Drawing on his experience as both an active participant within the financial industry and, more latterly, as a highly respected consultant, he walks us through the challenges we all confront in overcoming our reticence to ask challenging questions, and shows us how to do so effectively. The lessons in the book, however, are not confined to the narrow field of finance; anyone who is engaged in growing a business through client acquisition will relate to and learn from his particular wisdom.

Just Ask! is an apt and appropriate title. This is a book that all salespeople should own. If you want more high-quality clients, try asking for referrals. This excellent guide will show you how.

Brett Lankester
Former Chief Executive Officer, London,
Union Bancaire Privée

Key Takeaways

Client referrals provide numerous advantages over other methods for generating business: low effort yet high financial reward for you and your business, high hit ratio, lower anxiety, faster results **(Chapter 2)**.

Despite this, most people are reluctant to ask for referrals for many reasons **(Chapter 3)**. However, we can prepare ourselves to ask by improving our mindset and preparing our clients to receive the request for a referral more favourably **(Chapter 4)**. We increase our confidence **(Chapter 5)**, prepare ourselves to ask our clients **(Chapter 6)** and lead the conversation **(Chapter 7)**.

Making it easier for our client to make the referral not only increases the likelihood of success; it also makes it more natural for our client **(Chapter 8)**. In order to be effective, we must follow up without being pushy **(Chapter 9)**.

In Part Three, we look at other sources for referrals: existing and new intermediaries **(Chapter 10)**, friends and family **(Chapter 11)** and internal referrals **(Chapter 12)**.

Chapter 13 examines how to use networking and LinkedIn effectively and in the **Postscript**, we discuss 'asking in a pandemic'.

About the Author

Graham Eisner

Graham helps businesses of all shapes and sizes across all sectors and industries to achieve remarkable changes in their sales through referrals.

Over 20 years of delivering training and 10 years directly at Goldman Sachs, Graham has gained insights into psychological barriers and the reasons for success and failure from all the people he has trained and worked with. This gives him an unprecedented knowledge base about asking for referrals.

Graham worked at Goldman Sachs from 1990 to 2000 as a private client relationship manager. His primary role was to find clients and he became known internally as the group's expert on gaining referrals from internal partners, senior executives, clients and intermediaries.

Graham also ran the training programme for all Goldman Sachs' incoming private client salespeople in Europe. His experiences in these roles led him to create his own sales consultancy – focusing on the wealth advisory sector and other professional services industries – to train and mentor salespeople and their teams on how to increase referrals.

Graham has delivered hundreds of workshops on this subject using his methodologies.

Acknowledgements

I would like to acknowledge and thank the following people:

My wife **Selina**, who has been extremely supportive while I have been writing this book. Her clear mind and advice have always helped me to focus on what is important.

My business associate **Richard Clarke** for his always timely and precise advice.

Andrew Cave for his wealth of experience. He has helped me to position my thinking and my writing language in exactly the right direction to deliver this book.

Andrew Prescott for his excellent illustrations, which have made this business book much more colourful and enjoyable for the reader.

Tom Slocock, ex-Head of Wealth Management for Deutsche Bank in the UK, for some very important, timely advice while I was writing this book and for his valuable proofreading.

George Karolemeas for proofreading this book and helping me reformat certain parts to position it for a wider audience.

Simon Armstrong, ex-Head of Saltus Investment Management, for proofreading this book.

Frederick Kermisch, Sales Coach, for all his additions and work for this book. Frederick used his experience, both literary and industry-related, helping bankers to win new clients. Visit his website www.frederickkermisch.com to find out more about his work.

Finally, thanks to my brother **Alan Eisner** for, as always, some very direct and useful pointers for the book.

Part One

Don't Hold Back

Chapter 1

Why Ask?

Let's start with a word from Mark Zuckerberg, Founder and Chief Executive of Facebook: 'People influence people. Nothing influences people more than a recommendation from a trusted friend. A trusted referral influences people more than the best broadcast message. A trusted referral is the holy grail of advertising.'[1]

Referrals are a hidden gem. You're trying to grow your business using different methods, but missing this huge hidden pipeline of highly qualified prospects. This is the high-value prize on offer after you read this book.

You're a client adviser in the wealth management industry; or you might be a lawyer, accountant, sales consultant, entrepreneur or large enterprise account manager. The common denominator is that you all work with clients who are very valuable to you and your firm. These relationships are personal and strong; these clients trust, like and enjoy working with you. They are also loyal, respect and value the business you work in and pay well for the products and services you provide. Yet, despite all this, it never occurs to you to ask them for an introduction to another potential client who would also value your service or product. On the occasion when you do think of it, you find it difficult to ask for and receive the referral.

This is the huge conundrum that *Just Ask!* will solve.

---

[1] Available at: www.thetlinitiative.com/thought-leadership/word-of-mouth-referral-is-gold/

I worked as a private client salesperson for 10 years. Since 2001, I have trained salespeople in financial services and other professional service industries, entrepreneurs and enterprise account executives on how to increase business, specifically by asking for referrals. In this time, I believe I have heard virtually every reason as to why all these people working in sales do not ask. And I have witnessed hundreds of occasions where salespeople have accepted the power of asking for referrals. They have been motivated by my referral workshop to adopt this new methodology and ideas, but have then quickly reverted to their comfort zones, either not asking for referrals properly or not doing so at all. I have also witnessed success stories where individuals have been willing to change their belief system and apply this methodology, often with great success.

In this book, I am going to show you how to request business referrals in a strategic and planned-for manner. The reality is that one-third of success in asking for referrals simply comes from waking up to the fact that you *can* ask clients for referrals and you want to do so in order to grow your business. You will need to follow the process and stages that I describe, but it is not complicated.

How to use this book

- Many chapters include worksheets that will help you practise the ideas.
- You will find summary points of the main ideas at the end of each chapter.
- There is an appendix compiling all summary points at the end of the book. This section will efficiently remind you of the key takeaways of the book in the next months and years.

Due to my background in wealth management, this book primarily uses examples taken from my experience in this industry. The techniques work equally well in other industries that also value high-quality personal relationships, as successfully demonstrated by hundreds of my clients.

Throughout this book, when I refer to you (the reader), I acknowledge that not everyone views themselves as a 'salesperson'. A client adviser in the private banking world is of course selling their firm, resources and themselves. A lawyer reading this book may be dealing with clients, even though their role is not strictly about looking for more customers. An entrepreneur has a multifunctional role. An enterprise sales executive manages large strategic relationships for their firm. However, in all these roles, such people are always in some way selling their firm and themselves. They have a client-facing role, therefore, they're in a position to ask for a referral.

***

Fortunately, we live in times where the examples used in this book are applicable to all professionals, regardless of their gender. As such, he and she are used interchangeably in the book, as are male and female names. I trust the balance between readability and inclusivity is achieved.

A personal referrals experience

Let me tell you about my own credentials. I joined Goldman Sachs in 1990 in the private client area where the emphasis was on bringing in very wealthy people as clients. My focus was always on the easiest and most powerful way to find a new prospect and this is where referrals came in. My thought process was: 'Why not tap into the friends and business network of senior partners within Goldman Sachs to get personally referred prospects through the door?' My team could then do the rest in order to ensure that such prospects became clients, providing great service and trust early on in the relationship and introducing the right resources of the firm to meet their individual criteria and challenges.

After reading this book you will have the confidence to ask for a client referral in a comfortable manner. It does not matter if someone has been a client for one month, six months or 10 years; you can ask all clients. You can ask family and friends even if you are worried about uncomfortable conversations or crossing the line between business and home life. You can also ask former colleagues, business intermediaries and internal colleagues. This book will give you the tools to plan a strategy, to then ask for a referral and to monitor and follow up effectively, so that you capture all the benefits of the referral. I know from experience that if you follow the plan I describe, you will double your business.

If you're just starting out or have only a few clients, you're one of the lucky ones. Most of your senior, more experienced colleagues didn't take advantage of using referrals to build their businesses, instead taking harder and longer routes to finding new clients. By acquiring the habit of asking your precious clients for referrals early on in your career, you will benefit from the networking effect very quickly, with one referral leading to another as your clients understand that you build your business from referrals. This book will give you the early confidence, language and structure to create and execute a referral plan. This book will also help you think laterally about your contacts and become aware of many other possible routes whereby to ask for referrals and find new prospects.

You will not have to go down frustrating rabbit holes, waste time or experience the anxiety that is common among fledgling salespeople when they take on the wrong clients due to pressure from bosses to build their business quickly.

Of course, there will be other readers who don't have any clients yet. If you are one of them, I hope this book convinces you that asking for referrals is by far the quickest and easiest route to growing your business. You will have in front of you a list of contacts and opportunities to find prospects. By reading this book you will find tools to help you focus, prioritize and expand this list dramatically.

People just don't ask

Let me illustrate this with a story about one of the directors in a successful boutique firm for whom I ran a workshop. Before undertaking such sessions, I like to speak for about 30 minutes (over two short calls) with each participant one week before. I do this because I need the workshops to be as productive and commercially focused as possible. All attendees must come with a list of clients, intermediaries, family, friends and internal colleagues – their warmest opportunities to ask for referrals. On the call, therefore, I am asking participants to give me a sense of their business, how many clients they have and where referrals come from. On this occasion, the director said he had about 40 clients but, when asked how many he had personally asked for a referral, his honest answer was just one. Then, I asked him how many of his clients had actually given him referrals over a 10-year period. His answer was between 10 and 15.

Therein lay both a problem and an exciting opportunity. The director knew it too and that was why his firm had asked me to run the workshop. Clearly, he was skilled in his job, having won up to 15 referrals from satisfied clients. Yet the huge opportunities that he was missing were also evident. Each of the clients who had already given him referrals could be asked again, using the right language. After all, they had been happy to do so the first time around. Second, all the clients who came in from those initial referrals would also happily give referrals themselves, since this was their route to becoming clients in the first place. Third, think of all the other clients whom the director had never asked. They could definitely be asked to supply business referral opportunities too.

Think laterally

Even greater opportunities lie beyond the immediate scope of your client's own business relationships. Speaking to the director I just described, I also asked if any of his relationships with intermediaries, such as lawyers, accountants and trustees, had yielded referrals and he could only think of one firm that had done so. Asked to score how deeply this potential vein of new business had been mined, he gave it five out of 10, recognizing that, with some work, that single connection could produce many more referrals, as could his many other intermediary connections.

I then spoke to a second member of the firm, asking how many of her relatives or friends had been asked for referrals. The answer was none. When I asked whether there were any such people who could refer, if asked in the right way, she said there were probably between one and three. Pressed further, she said that probably all three could be approached successfully. Thinking strategically like this provided great material to work with in the workshop and the opportunities mentioned duly led to new business.

A willingness to change

You will be motivated by this book and you will want to change, but to actually do so will take real work. Human memory is short and can act like an elastic band, so even when you have plucked up the confidence to follow the steps I describe for converting a potential opportunity into a successful business referral, that elastic band will take you back to your previous ways of operating, with their restrictive thought patterns, fears and mindsets.

It takes effort to change such mindsets, but it becomes easier when people remember the reasons for doing so and the benefits, and when they are shown how to do so in a way that limits any risk.

Chapter 1:

Summary Points

Why ask?

Referrals are a hidden gem. This book will give you the individual strategies to double your business.

Currently:

- **You find it difficult to ask.**
- **You forget to ask.**
- **You are unsure how to ask.**

This book will give you:

- **a strategy for each client/intermediary;**
- **the confidence to ask;**
- **methods to think laterally; and**
- **a willingness and motivation to change.**

How to maximize your use of this book:

- **Use the worksheets to exercise your memory and new habits.**
- **Use the summary points to re-visit and engage with your new-found methodology.**

The Number One Strategy

Client referrals must be the number one choice for finding new clients

The power of word-of-mouth as a source of new business was emphatically expressed by Tony Hsieh, Chief Executive of Zappos 2009–2020: 'We take most of the money that we could have spent on paid advertising and instead put it back into the customer experience. Then we let the customer be our marketing. Historically, our number one growth driver has been from repeat customers and word-of-mouth.'[2]

When I ask how firms attempt to recruit new clients, a majority say that they will pay for talented salespeople who have an established client base, buy a competing company for their client base or invest in a marketing strategy. Some companies will pay existing clients in some form to be able to use their name as a testimonial. Others will sponsor events, arrange dinners and entertainment to attract potential clients and give them the chance to touch and feel their products, services, people and DNA.

Such strategies all have a financial cost, but also take up a great deal of time in planning and organizing; they also do not guarantee success, despite the heavy financial investment and time required. Asking for client referrals, on the other hand, is close to being free, takes virtually no time and, if unsuccessful, costs you nearly nothing.

---

[2] Available at: www.forbes.com/2010/07/01/tony-hsieh-zappos-leadership-managing-interview.html?sh=79bbe4146d4e

In this chapter, we will review some of the advantages of using referrals as a business acquisition strategy. You will understand why using referrals is my preferred method for acquiring business.

Referrals are the number one strategy to grow your client base and business for the following key reasons.

One Referral Leads to Many

1. **Referrals reduce the anxiety of finding new business and reduce the pricing pressure on fees from a prospect**

   Reducing anxiety as to the source of your next clients provides a major incentive to implement a much more effective referrals programme within your company. But there is also another powerful hidden reason why referrals make so much sense. The very act of your being introduced to a friend, business colleague or intermediary means that the client undertaking the introduction likes and trusts you and thinks you can be of genuine value to the person they are putting you in touch with. This means there will be far less pricing pressure or bargaining down of fees within the new relationship, compared to other less personal ways of finding clients.

   Thanks to the fact that your client has already decided that your pricing is right, she will be able to explain why she recommends your services and the benefits you provide. As such, the discussion with the new prospect is more likely to focus on potential benefits than on your fees.

2. **Referrals are easier and quicker to close than other methods of procuring new business**

   The other benefit of asking for a referral is that it carries a much greater likelihood of your being able to rapidly convert a prospect into a client. If prospects have had your services personally recommended to them, they enter communications with you much further along the line of saying 'yes' than if they had met you via a different route. The benefits of this should not be underestimated. Time saved in finding new clients and bringing them on board could equal a day or more. This can compound as weeks saved for a higher return on investment. Remember, the by-product of all this is that the growth rate for your business will be much faster, with a higher quality of client because you have already effectively qualified (defined and narrowed down) the sort of referral that you are looking for.

3. Referrals make valuable use of a powerful networking effect

Correctly enabled and carried out, personal client referrals become a naturally recurring phenomenon because of the networking effect. Once you have got a referral from a client, you can easily ask this client for another referral at some point. Second, this newly referred client understands that you build your business successfully through referrals because that is their exact experience of it. Therefore, it will be completely natural for you – at the right moment – to also ask them for a referral. They already understand how another contact of theirs has been looked after by you and your firm. Trust is already there in abundance and they have also experienced your superior products and services, interactions, decision-making and mode of operating.

4. Referrals increase the loyalty of the existing client who is giving the referral

Giving you a referral will also increase your existing client's loyalty because the decision to give you a referral will have involved some ego and emotion. Your existing client has invested further in you by making a referral and this is likely to increase their own loyalty to you as they will want to prove to themselves that they made the right decision. If tough conditions appear for your existing client, it is less likely that they will cease to be a client.

5. **Referrals increase your enjoyment of your job**
   We all want to enjoy the work of the business we are in, but this idea can be forgotten to some extent and it is really important not to let that happen. The clients you have and how you get on with them clearly have an effect on the enjoyment, motivation, energy and passion you have for your products and services. As referrals more often than not lead to you working with more like-minded people, you are therefore increasing the enjoyment of your job.

Chapter 2:

Summary Points

The number one strategy

Why referrals should be the number one strategy to grow your business:

- **Referrals reduce your costs of acquisition of new business.**
- **Referrals reduce your anxiety about finding new business.**
- **Referrals help you focus on high-probability prospects, thereby reducing time wasted.**

Ask yourself:

How much anxiety and stress stem from the way you currently try to find new clients?

How many new prospects have you truly acquired from the methods you use?

How much time have you spent in doing so?

- **Referrals mean less pricing pressure from an incoming referred client.**
- **Referred prospects are easier and quicker to close.**
- **There is a networking effect. Clients who have been referred will themselves refer.**
- **Referrals increase the loyalty of existing clients who give a referral.**
- **Referrals increase the enjoyment in your job.**

Chapter 3

Why People Don't Ask

The importance of going for what you want is summed up by Nora Roberts, author of more than 220 novels: 'If you don't go after what you want, you'll never have it. If you don't ask, the answer is always "no". If you don't step forward, you're always in the same place.'[3] Many clients would actually love to be asked for a referral, feeling flattered at the request and honoured to be able to help you. I have heard it commonly said that, while salespeople only ask for referrals from 20% of their clients, 60% of their client base would actually be happy to offer them one.

This chapter will examine the mindsets and specific beliefs that hold you back from asking for referrals. Until we realize which beliefs are holding us back, we are likely to find excuses to avoid changing our behaviour. Examining and addressing the most common fears make it easier to adopt new successful behaviours. It can be easy to assume that people will naturally make referrals. However, in my experience, people easily overlook even the most obvious referrals, and are often grateful when we help them bring these about.

1. **People don't agree with their importance**
    One fundamental mindset that blocks the use of referrals is that some people just do not really see

---

[3] Available at: www.goodreads.com/author/quotes/625.Nora_ Roberts

the importance of them. It is a silently ignored topic. People get too busy to plan and strategize properly around asking for referrals. It is not an innate client-facing skill, so it gets ignored. New business is staring everyone in the face, but they do not really see the value in it. If it was seen as important, there would be more training devoted to both external and internal client referrals.

2. The subconscious fear of rejection
It is clear that many people find it really difficult to ask for referrals and of course psychological reasons come into the business relationship here. Asking invites rejection, and fear of rejection holds us back from advancing in business, just as it does in private personal relationships. If you feel strongly that a product or service would help someone and exert time and effort trying to convince them of this, you are using the business part of your brain, and speaking persuasively will hopefully lead to a new client. But asking for a referral is emotive. In your brain, it starts to test whether a particular client likes and trusts you and thinks you do a good job for them. It is only natural to care deeply about such matters. You may also have been rejected in your own personal life by family, friends or in a romantic relationship and this plays subconsciously into your business life.

This is vulnerability at its core. By asking for a referral, you are becoming vulnerable, and as humans, we all run away from these feelings of vulnerability. Therefore, we prefer to keep the status quo and not ask. If this resonates with you, this is not a problem in itself. Indeed, recognizing the fact can be a first stage in not letting it get in the way of asking for a referral for business reasons. Following the advice of this book will help you get to a zone during client meetings where you are unaffected by these feelings, or at least know how to switch them off.

Psychologically, there is not much difference between the fear of rejection and the fear of physical danger. This goes a long way to explain why we are so averse to possibly exposing ourselves to rejection.

3. We forget to ask

There is no reminder to ask for a referral; we just simply get too busy with other things and forget to ask in the client meeting. Of course, first of all, this is connected to the fact that we have many blocks to asking, so on a subconscious basis we simply forget. We forget because we have covered so many other issues in the presentation that we do not have the time to cover this. We forget because we do not see the importance of asking for referrals, and we do not want to ask. There is no historical evidence of people doing this very successfully in the business, so we simply also forget. Forgetting might simply be a convenient excuse to stay in our comfort zone, even though this is probably costing us a significant sum of easily available money.

Mindsets that stop us asking

Below is a long but not necessarily exhaustive list of specific beliefs that may resonate with you.

- I am too chummy with him. Having worked with him for 20 years and never asked for a referral, suddenly asking for one will make him think I am a different person.

- My client has such a long list of possible referrals that I don't know how to start.
- I will get rejected.
- This client is not well connected, too old, too young and doesn't mix in the right circles.
- I have not known this client long enough to ask.
- The client is a nervous, intense character, so asking for a referral feels like too much of an uphill challenge.
- It will be an uncomfortable situation, so I prefer not to ask.
- I don't really like this client. Their character is quite difficult so it gets in the way of me asking. I also fear that I will be referred to another client like them.
- I have a number of clients who all know each other. They are great clients but awkward to ask. If I ask one or two, they will mention it to each other and will then be expecting it, which will be embarrassing.
- I just do not have time with existing client demands and work life to be asking for referrals.
- I think the client has not been happy with my service, so I don't want to ask.
- They will give me a referral anyway, so I don't need to ask.
- I worry it will open up a 'Pandora's box' and they will start to tell me negative things about our relationship.
- I asked them recently and don't want to ask them again.
- When I have asked before, the client said they would introduce Mr/Mrs X but it did not happen, so I don't feel that confident about asking again.
- They are too busy.

- When we have a meeting, we have so little time that I can't ask about this. It would be wrong. The meeting and relationship are for them, not me.
- I'm too junior to ask. Or I have taken on clients from a previous salesperson.
- I feel that it's too 'salesy' or pushy to ask.
- I don't know how to ask.
- The administration is so onerous in our firm that we don't have time to ask for referrals or deliver on them.
- I never meet the client in person.

Overcoming Negative Mindsets

What I want to do now is illustrate why each of these mindsets should not hold you back. If you don't have an answer for your particular mindset, please email me with your mindset at graham@graham-eisner.com and I will respond personally.

1. **I am too chummy with him. Having worked with him for 20 years and never asked for a referral, suddenly asking for one will make him think I am a different person.**
    This situation is perfect for a referral as the client knows you extremely well. There are client situations where you are overly sensitive about how you are viewed in their eyes. You worry that they know you as a certain type of person who has worked with them for many years and that suddenly asking for something will make you look like somebody else entirely. You have worked hard to create this personal impression and are concerned that acting differently now could change the relationship. This is an understandable feeling but it is completely in your mind and does not necessarily reflect the truth. You are friends with this client but there is also a business relationship there, even if it does not feel that way. The client definitely views it this way, as your firm is providing valuable services. Most importantly the client would love to help you. You just need to ask.

2. **My client has such a long list of possible referrals that I don't know how to start.**
    This is what one might describe as a high-quality problem. It is actually about motivation and language. If you really do see the amazing opportunity here, and I hope that after reading this book, you can and will, we must find a way for you to break this pattern.

Try something like: 'Rachel, there is something I need to ask your help with and I will bring it up in our next meeting.' Then use the language recommended in this book to bring up asking for a referral, working through the list of those whom your client can ask and the most appropriate follow-up strategy.

3. I will get rejected.

The way to look at this is to ask: 'What is really the worst that can happen?' If you do ask and they refuse, you have not lost anything. The situation is exactly as it was. In personal relationships, we can work ourselves up to thinking a problem exists when it never did. It is the same with asking for a referral. We can think that the client will notice the fact that you brought up this question again and again after a meeting and it will affect your long-term relationship. But let's be honest; clients are usually thinking about themselves and not about you and what you just asked.

4. This client is not well connected, too old, too young and doesn't mix in the right circles.

We often make assumptions about our clients but don't know the truth about them. They could be timid, unsociable, extremely private or too old. But, of course, none of the above suggests that they are completely unconnected and also, as you will see later, we are only going to ask for *one* referral. They will probably know one person who could be a good client referral for you. And if they don't, what is the downside? Is there really a risk that you will have damaged the relationship?

5. **I have not known this client long enough to ask.**
   What makes you say you haven't known this client
   long enough? What constitutes long enough? I could
   have known a client for one week but spent a lot of
   time with them in that period. That would be long
   enough to ask them for a referral. Alternatively, I could
   have known them for 10 years and yet met them only
   five times. The better questions therefore are: Do they
   like you? Do they trust you? Do they appreciate the
   values of your firm and the services you offer them?
   If the answers to these questions are positive, then you
   can ask them for a referral whether you have known
   them for a week, a month or a year. What is important
   is that when you ask, you ask in a very professional and
   methodical way, something we will discuss a little later
   in the book.

6. **The client is a nervous, intense character, so**
   asking for a referral feels like too much of an
   uphill challenge.
   This is where the use of words is important and when
   and how we ask. If you can break away for a minute
   or two from the client business situation, slow your
   voice, soften your tone and calmly and profession-
   ally ask for help on one thing, you will find that they
   will disassociate from how they normally behave and
   move into being more willing to help you.

7. **It will be an uncomfortable situation, so I prefer**
   not to ask.
   Again, this is uncomfortable only in your mind. Why
   should it be uncomfortable? Challenge yourself and
   ask why this will be uncomfortable. This is a projec-
   tion. You feel uneasy so you think your client will

be too. In your mind there is a concern that you are putting your client in a difficult situation. But you are not asking to know the exact background of their friend or business colleague, or for them to find it out. They will make a fair assumption from what they know, be happy to help you and make an introduction. Nothing more complicated than that needs to occur. I suggest that, with this mindset, you are making the situation more complicated than it needs to be.

You might want to ask yourself whether you believe the situation will be uncomfortable for you or for your client. If you are concerned that it will be uncomfortable for you but not for your client, maybe think from your client's perspective: is it possible she will actually welcome your question? If so, why deprive her by not asking it? Don't let your own discomfort determine how you behave with your clients, especially if it means depriving them of the chance to grant a favour they might be happy to give.

8. **I don't really like this client. Their character is quite difficult and gets in the way of me asking. I also fear that I will be referred to another client like them.**

Clearly, this is a legitimate thought. However, if we stand back from this for a second, the person they introduce could be someone they know through work or socially, but in no way do they need to be like the person referring them. That is clearly something in your head. As in many of these situations, they will appreciate how you deal with them and will probably be very happy to give you a referral. Probably, they are difficult in all their relationships. We need to separate how we feel about them as a client and the fact that they may give a good referral. Remember that receiving a referral does not mean that the person will become your client. Nor does it mean that you are forced to accept them as a client. If you feel you will not enjoy having someone as a client, you can turn them down. Having the option to accept them might be better than having no option at all.

9. **I have a number of clients who all know each other. They are great clients but awkward to ask. If I ask one or two, they will mention it to each other and will then be expecting it, which will be embarrassing.**

We assume that people like to talk about us and what we are doing, but most of the time that is not what they are talking about. In this situation, it is the language you use that is all-important. Start with one of the clients, saying you are looking to grow the business slowly and that this is a great group where you want to ask each member individually, but you want to start with them. This situation can be turned around so that each member of this group actually becomes a key introducer to your firm. It is about recognizing all the value that you offer to these clients.

10. **I just do not have time with existing client demands and work life to be asking for referrals.**

This is where I would ask all my readers to look honestly at their business and see what time is normally wasted in an average day. Time management is key. What could you do differently to free up time in your day? Structure your days, question the validity of all external and internal meetings and ask yourself how many clients you have and how many really are not worth your time. How organized are you and what could improve? How good are you at using resources, both from the firm and from your team? How good is the division of roles on the team? These are just a few questions, but I am going to bet that asking them will enable you to save 20% of your time. Think what time this then frees up for activity to grow your business, including creation of a sensible and realistic referral strategy.

11. I think the client has not been happy with my service, so I don't want to ask.

How are they unhappy with the service? Is it just a short-term blip? Are they really unhappy? Is this just in your mind? Some clients often complain, look unhappy and express frustration about products and services. Do you really know that they are unhappy and, if they were, wouldn't it be good to address this anyway? If you step back a second and look at how long they have been a client, perhaps the relationship has been going for many years and this slight unhappiness is a very small blip. If so, they would still react very favourably if you asked for a referral. And if it is something major, you will probably have to deal with this eventually. You might be better off dealing with it earlier to avoid the risk of losing the client.

12. They will give me a referral anyway, so I don't need to ask.

This is one of the most common mistakes people make. They get on very well with their client or have even developed a friendship. They know the client really likes them and speaks favourably about them. They are therefore convinced that the client is thinking about them and will make a referral to them when they have somebody in mind. As much as a client might like you, however, they are unlikely to give you a referral if you don't ask for one. That means that this is a lost opportunity. The client would absolutely give you a client referral if you asked in the right way.

And yes, you might be right, they might give you a referral without being asked. But have they done it before? If not, what leads you to believe or hope that they will do it now without a bit of prodding?

13. I worry it will open up a 'Pandora's box' and they will start to tell me negative things about our relationship.

What are you really saying here? Are you perceiving something that is untrue? Is it in your character to think negatively and always see a downside? Or are you nervous that there are actually some negative things that your client would raise? Again, would it not be best to deal with such issues anyway for the sake of your long-term relationship? If they have something negative to say, isn't it better that they say it to you rather than to someone else? If the criticism is valid, take it on board. And if it is unreasonable, it is better to have a clearer image of what they are thinking.

14. I asked them recently and don't want to ask them again.

First, it is great that you asked. What happened? Did you get a good referral? Or do you not want to ask again because they gave you a bad referral or it was an uncomfortable situation? We will cover this in Chapter 7, as it is very important to define the sort of referral you actually want. However, the fact is that they were keen to offer you a referral recently, whether that was one, three or six months or a year ago. If you word another request in the right way, it can be very reasonable to do so. It is not as if the last referral they gave was only two weeks ago. You could easily say that some capacity has recently opened up in your business and ask for their help in potentially filling it.

15. When I have asked before, the client said they would introduce Mr/Mrs X but it did not happen, so I don't feel that confident about asking again.

I don't know how you asked last time, but I would urge you to put that behind you and consider whether you could ask this client for another referral. Perhaps it was the way you asked or how you followed up. In other words, the reasons for the client not following through and not making it happen do not need to be a reason not to ask again. Remember, this might be one of your best clients who really wants to help you. Is it possible they simply forgot and will be grateful that you jolted their memory? And if they changed their mind, you might be better off knowing.

16. They are too busy.

Once again, this is your perception of your client. They may always come across as very busy and maybe this is true, but how do you know they would not be very happy to help you by making an introduction? They may be very busy but also very generous to others. If you don't ask, you will never get. Outside all this, there is nothing unprofessional about asking. If you ask politely and they say they are too busy to focus on this right now, just tell them that is fine but would they mind if you ask them again in six months' time?

Finally, on this point of being too busy, this whole business of asking for a referral really takes about three minutes (maximum) of their time, so it is not a lot. It requires a shift in mindset from your side. We will outline later a comfortable way to ask which also makes it clear that this will be something a client can do for you really quickly.

17. **When we have a meeting, we have so little time that I cannot ask about this. It would be wrong. The meeting and relationship are for them, not me.** Your perception is that the meetings are so tight for time that you really do not have the time to ask. In reality, this request will take up only three minutes of the meeting. I would ask how efficient you are in managing the meeting time. How choreographed are meetings before you start to achieve what you have planned? Again, if you choose your moment well and ask efficiently in a meeting, it should be no problem to ask. The focus of the meeting, of course, is on your client. However, there is always room to make a three-minute request. If we are honest with ourselves, this is a great excuse not to ask. It actually means that you would never ask this client, as meetings will always be busy and tight. But this client might be one of the best advocates for your product and services, with an extremely suitable contact who could benefit, so you really do have to find a way to ask them.

18. I am too junior to ask. Or I have taken on clients from a previous salesperson.

In this situation, I recommend meeting the previous salesperson and asking them about each individual client, how the relationship was, how well the client appreciated the services of your firm, and if they were asked for a referral. When you are asking for a referral, remember that they are giving a referral to the firm and not to you. Therefore, it is always important to speak about your firm. If you speak about the DNA, culture, credibility and services and resources of the firm and move the subject away from you, it is very reasonable to expect them to give you a referral. You are a conduit to all these attributes of the firm. Accordingly, it does not matter if you are new to the job, young, junior, inexperienced or have just taken on this client from a former salesperson. What's more important is how you talk about the firm and bring these resources to your client. If you do this, you will get the referral. How much experience would be enough for you to feel comfortable about asking? Sometimes feeling 'too junior' is a convenient excuse to procrastinate and avoid an uncomfortable situation.

19. I feel that it's too 'salesy' or pushy to ask.

Anyone who has built a business has asked people on their journey for help and advice. We need to define what is being pushy or 'salesy'. You are not being aggressive, obnoxious or rude or crossing the boundaries of what is appropriate for a client–salesperson relationship. In fact, you are being professional, assertive and confident about what you want. Clients actually respect this. It is also worth stepping back for a second and asking if anyone has ever said that you are pushy on a business or personal level. I am going to guess that the answer is 'no'. It is powerful to realize that asking for a referral will not be deemed pushy if you ask in the right way.

When people talk about being pushy or 'salesy', they sometimes mean 'not taking no for an answer' or 'doing anything to get a yes, even being misleading or deceiving'. I assume that you do neither of these things. Simply asking a straightforward question does not run a risk of you seeming pushy or 'salesy'.

20. I don't know how to ask.
Fair enough. Why should you know how to ask or how to ask successfully? There are nuances to this. We will cover how to ask in Chapters 6, 7, 8 and 9. Ask yourself: 'If you knew how to ask, would there be any other reasons not to ask?' If yes, what are they?

21. The administration is so onerous in our firm that we don't have time to ask for referrals or deliver on them.
I do understand and respect this. In every firm, there are always time-wasting internal rules and paperwork that hold you back from being able to get new business. However, to enter into the referral mindset and be successful, we have to be positive and confident and not find things that, if we are honest, are forms of procrastination.

22. I never meet the client in person.
How long have you known this person? How close are you? How close would you really need to be to feel comfortable asking for a referral? Do you always achieve what you need to over the phone or by email?

In other words, you probably have a good client relationship and therefore no worries at all about asking successfully for a referral. I am assuming you cannot meet because you are not in the same city or area. Clearly, in the post-COVID-19 world, this may become the norm for some clients anyway. However, if you are not likely to meet, I suggest that you can ask for the referral remotely. Please note that this should be only on the phone, not via email. It is important to hear the response to your request and be able to respond there and then to it, as if you were meeting face-to-face.

Exercise

Make a list of your clients. For each client, think about the specific mindset that is holding you back from asking for a referral. Fill in the columns on the following worksheet. Refer to the examples above to help you work out which mindsets you are applying to each client.

The temptation will be to do this quickly and conclude that it is a similar mindset for each client. However, I guarantee that this is not the case and the exercise is well worth the time. The clarity provided by this exercise will give you the confidence to definitely be able to ask and get around the mindset that has been holding you back.

***

After filling in this mindset worksheet, ask yourself:

- What patterns of mindsets keep coming up?
- What has surprised you?
- Are you finding excuses not to ask?

Discuss these reactions with a buddy.

WORKSHEET

Mindsets that are holding you back from asking for referrals

1. I am too chummy with him. Having worked with him for 20 years and never asked for a referral, suddenly asking for one will make him think I am a different person.

2. My client has such a long list of possible referrals that I don't know how to start.

3. I will get rejected.

4. This client is not well connected, too old, too young and doesn't mix in the right circles.

5. I have not known this client long enough to ask.

6. The client is a nervous, intense character, so asking for a referral feels like too much of an uphill challenge.

7. It will be an uncomfortable situation, so I prefer not to ask.

8. I don't really like this client. Their character is quite difficult so it gets in the way of me asking. I also fear that I will be referred to another client like them.

9. I have a number of clients who all know each other. They are great clients but awkward to ask. If I ask one or two, they will mention it to each other and will then be expecting it, which will be embarrassing.

10. I just do not have time with existing client demands and work life to be asking for referrals.

11. I think the client has not been happy with my service, so I don't want to ask.

12. They will give me a referral anyway, so I don't need to ask.

13. I worry it will open up a 'Pandora's box' and they will start to tell me negative things about our relationship.

14. I asked them recently and don't want to ask them again.

15. When I have asked before, the client said they would introduce Mr/Mrs X but it did not happen, so I don't feel that confident about asking again.

16. They are too busy.

17. When we have a meeting, we have so little time that I cannot ask about this. It would be wrong. The meeting and relationship are for them, not me.

18. I'm too junior to ask. Or I have taken on clients from a previous salesperson.

19. I feel that it's too 'salesy' or pushy to ask.

20. I don't know how to ask.

21. The administration is so onerous in our firm that we don't have time to ask for referrals or deliver on them.

22. I never meet the client in person.

Client name	Specific mindsets holding you back

Hopefully now you have a positive mindset towards asking for referrals.

Please now use the following worksheet to help you create a focused list of where your priority client referrals could come from.

WORKSHEET

Create a prioritized client referral list

Go through your list of clients and under each point add the client names.

   1. Clients who trust and like you the most:
   -
   -
   -
   -
   -
   -
   -
   -
   -
   -

   2. Most valuable clients in terms of revenue:
   -
   -
   -
   -
   -
   -
   -
   -
   -
   -

3. Clients with most potential regardless of revenue:

-
-
-
-
-
-
-
-
-
-

4. Clients who have referred a prospect to you before:

-
-
-
-
-
-
-
-
-

5. Clients whom you know are networked and very connected:

-
-
-
-
-
-
-
-
-

6. Clients who for some reason have really benefited from the firm's resources, values and USPs:

-
-
-
-
-
-
-
-
-
-

Based on the previous answers, complete the following:

Tier 1: 10 clients with highest likelihood to provide referrals:

-
-
-
-
-
-
-
-
-
-

Tier 2: Next 10 clients with high likelihood to provide referrals:
-
-
-
-
-
-
-
-
-
-

Tier 3: 10 more clients with a likelihood to provide referrals:
-
-
-
-
-
-
-
-
-
-

Chapter 3:

Summary Points

Why people don't ask

While people in sales only ask for referrals from 20% of their clients, 60% of their client base would actually be happy to offer them one.

Why we don't ask for referrals:

- **We don't agree with their importance.**
- **We have a subconscious fear of rejection.**
- **We forget to ask.**

Our mindset gets in the way of asking:

- **Fear on many levels leads to procrastination.**
- **We make assumptions about clients and their reactions.**
- **We are too confident that referrals will simply be given.**

All these mindsets are in our heads and none of them need hold us back from asking for a referral.

Create a prioritized client referral list.

Make It Easier for Yourself

Making It Easier to Ask for Referrals

1 Manage your time effectively

2 Improve client service

3 Be proud of your USPs

4 Practise positive thinking

5 Use your buddy
To help monitor progress

Let's begin with some words of wisdom from Lao Tzu, the ancient Chinese philosopher and writer: 'Do the difficult things while they are easy and do the great things while they are small. A journey of a thousand miles must begin with a single step.'[4] Before we embark on the journey of creating a referral strategy for each client, we must do all we can to ensure that, once we start, the possibility of success is at the maximum. I know the industries this book has been written for and I also know that the salespeople who will read this book are good at what they do. They are hard-working, with good communication skills. They have had a good deal of training in sales and they do think seriously about how to serve their clients as effectively as possible and deliver at a high level. They are genuine and authentic and have the long-term gains of their clients in mind.

This chapter will suggest some quick wins to make asking for referrals more natural, and therefore more easy and more likely to be successful.

What can make it easier to ask for and receive a referral? Enhance your service to clients

Clearly a happy client is one who is more likely to give a referral; a client who feels that the relationship is a good one and that they have received good service, follow-up and hand-holding in times that are hard.

None of the above is hard to imagine. The real question for today is: 'What can you improve with your clients?' This is not a general question. What I would like you to do now

---

[4] Available from: www.goodreads.com/quotes/668317-do-the-difficult-things-while-they-are-easy-and-do

is go through your client list and, against each name, list one thing you could improve that would be valuable and relevant for your client.

The worksheet below uses the following list:

- Service
- Contact
- Hand-holding
- Following up
- Bringing the right resources of the firm to benefit your client
- Care and attention
- Time
- Education about the products.

WORKSHEET

List all clients and the specific areas of the relationship that need to be improved for you to be comfortable in asking for a referral; e.g., service, follow-up, hand-holding, access to resources.

Make it easier to ask for referrals

Client	Main areas to improve

You will know what the area is for each client and, as we know, it will be different for each client. You can still ask a client for a referral without the needed improvements that you have selected above. However, the outcome could be a better response and success rate if you have improved in at least one of the areas.

Empowering yourself

What you will have seen up to now is that there are many reasons why we do not ask for referrals. One of the main reasons is that the subconscious mind is holding us back; the negative thoughts that we are serving ourselves. What I am about to say is something you might relate to on a personal basis; it also occurs in business. We feel we have no control over our thoughts.

Negative thoughts related to referrals might be:

- I am uncomfortable around referrals.
- I don't think I am very good at asking.
- I won't succeed in asking for referrals.
- I can think of an easier way to build my business.

These are negative thoughts and lead to a downward spiral around asking for referrals. We consciously need to think positively, such as:

- I am good at asking for referrals.
- I am comfortable asking for referrals.
- I am excited to see my business grow from asking for referrals.
- I will make the time to ask for referrals and strategize for each client on how to ask.

- My client is happy to give me referrals.

Try it. You will notice the difference in your approach to referrals.

The other way in which the mind is working negatively concerns questions you ask yourself to think about, such as:

- Why am I not good at asking for referrals?
- Why don't I like asking for referrals?
- Why are referrals not a bigger part of my business?
- Why do I find it so difficult to ask for referrals?
- Why does everyone find it difficult?
- Why don't I succeed in asking for referrals?

The point is that your brain will always be looking to find an answer to the questions you ask it. If you ask questions like the ones above – all questions with a negative connotation – your brain will automatically find reasons that are negative. This goes on to feed on itself negatively and basically delivers on what you are thinking. Your thinking becomes your norm and your reality.

However, you can turn this around by asking positive questions to which your brain will only find positive answers. The opposite will then occur. Positive answers will become the norm and feed on themselves. Suddenly you will feel strong and positive towards referrals.

***

Try asking yourself questions such as:

- Why are referrals so useful for my business?
- How can I be good at asking for referrals?
- Why, particularly for me, are referrals a perfect method to grow my business?
- My business is set up for referrals. Why is that?
- My clients think I am great. Why should asking for referrals work for me?
- What's positive about asking for referrals?
- Why is asking for referrals in meetings easy?
- Why do I think I deserve referrals?
- Why do I think a client would like to give me referrals?
- How can I become better at asking for referrals?
- What works well when asking for referrals?

Changing how the brain works towards asking for referrals

Our brains work on repeat cycles. There are neural pathways that are defined and called upon again and again, and often they are operating subconsciously. So, the pathways that raise negatives, or difficulties around mindsets, will come up, and then the thoughts associated with those will be on a loop and repeated. They will reinforce the negatives and the negative thinking.

I have already mentioned that one way to challenge this is through empowering thoughts, as these train your brain to find different answers and therefore solutions. However, another way is thinking of or creating positive scenarios around asking for referrals, and then nurturing the seed that led to this positive result or action.

- How did you approach a meeting differently regarding asking for a referral?
- What did you do, say and feel differently?
- How did you react differently to a client's actions or reactions?
- What did you appreciate at the time about the way it went when you had this interaction with a client?
- What were you grateful for?
- What can you bottle and keep for next time to ensure that you experience the same feelings?

When you create positive scenarios in this way, you are taking control of your mind and helping your brain work for you. Of course, this takes effort and practice, but the benefits are great. With practice, you will rewire this referral neural pathway and be able to walk into a meeting in a different place in your head. You will then approach asking for referrals with a different mentality.

To combine these two approaches, start by using empowering questions, as described. Let this switch your brain to positive thinking about referrals. Then think back to a meeting where it worked and carry out the above suggestions.

Appreciate the values and unique selling propositions (USPs) that you offer to clients

The idea of appreciating and believing in the values and USPs that you offer to clients will be affected by your cultural background. I hope American readers will not mind me saying here that they are typically bold and very comfortable in appreciating their own achievements and saying that they are doing a good job. The British, meanwhile, often have a shy modesty around the job they do and do not fully appreciate the value that they offer. What's important in starting to ask for referrals is really to believe in both the value that you offer and the value that comes from the resources of your firm.

This was very evident in a workshop I organized where a financial firm recognized that it had spent a lot of time discussing its brand, USPs and the importance of improving its website, but did not expressly take pride in what it had achieved when in front of clients.

This company's values include:

- what they deliver for clients;
- peace of mind for their clients;
- clarity;
- making clients feel very comfortable;
- planning, rather than selling;
- helping clients fulfil their goals;
- acting as a sounding board;
- the client being in safe hands; and
- providing great education and technical knowledge that clients can understand.

In order to help you think more deeply about your firm's values and USPs, consider the following:

- What is your process of doing business?
- How does your business model work?
- What is the public/private ownership mix of your business?

- What is your business structure and how does it deliver for clients?
- How bespoke are your products and services?
- Is your approach aggressive or conservative?
- To what extent is the success of your firm's methodology due to it taking on complex issues or trying to keep matters simple?
- How does your firm exhibit honesty, integrity and authenticity?
- Does your firm truly apply its people and services towards serving clients over the long term?

It is important for everyone to sit back and let the values and USPs of their business seep into their souls. If you can feel this, you will have no modesty around asking for a referral. This is what will make a big shift in your mind – realizing how valuable it is for someone else, the friend or colleague of your client, also to receive these values. By making an introduction, your client is providing a real service for their friend or colleague. Likewise, you are performing a service to your client by giving them the opportunity to do this.

WORKSHEET

Values and USPs of your firm

What sets your firm apart from the competition?

Values and USPs of your firm

Organize your time better

Time management is obviously a big topic for all businesses and there is a lot of advice on this. On the one hand, it is helpful to realize the inherent value of an hour of your time. Before you invest an hour in some activity, think of the monetary value of this hour. Would you be willing to spend the money? If not, maybe think twice before spending (investing?) the time. It may be easy to spend an hour browsing through emails but harder to justify spending a few hundred dollars to browse through emails. This simple trick can make it easier to avoid meetings that would be a waste of time. It can also help us identify low-quality prospects and think twice before randomly investing hours in chasing them. This is another powerful example of why referrals as a business-generation tool produce a high return on a low investment.

This also means delegating tasks that can be delegated; outsourcing tasks that can be outsourced. Furthermore, creating the best possible environment for successful work does make a difference. Exercising reduces stress, and improves energy and focus. Planning each day and being more tidy and better organized may not seem like much. But it is under our control and over time makes a significant difference to the results we produce.

The list is long and I could continue. The reality is that with all of the above, you are in control. We tell ourselves, both consciously and subconsciously, that our degree of control is much less than it actually is, but that is not really true. Take each of the above points and ask yourself honestly: 'Is this me? Could I improve it, and how?' I am certain you could come up with some good ways to improve.

The point is that if you are able to improve on a number of these areas, you will have strategic time to go and build your business. How you then go about building your business is also under your control. What I am advocating in this book is that you focus strategically on referrals, concentrating on each client or intermediary individually to find opportunities for referrals. Time spent on this will be very well rewarded.

How can you organize your time better and have more time to focus on planning referrals, executing them well and following up?

- Reduce time on the other strategies you currently use to find more clients.
- Prioritize your referral opportunities.
- Create a spreadsheet to monitor and follow up your referral opportunities (see the worksheet in Chapter 9).
- Work out which existing clients or intermediaries you are wasting time with.
- Can you reorganize your day somehow: for example, by allotting yourself strategic time for emailing and administration? Should you redefine roles within your team?

Get a buddy system working to help you

I know you are motivated to increase your referrals by the fact that you picked up this book. And, of course, some of you will work through it diligently and think about what I am suggesting and try to use it. My experience with training of any kind is that you have to practise what you have learnt at least five times for it to start having an effect and for the training to sink in.

After leading workshops, I always speak to most of the participants on a one-to-one basis, as my formula is to be hands-on and work through the referral opportunities with clients to ensure that they happen. The aim here is policing the learning, keeping people accountable and helping them succeed. Generally, it works well. However, when I organize role-play with attendees on the day of a meeting when they are going to ask for a referral, it never ceases to amaze me that they fail to remember some of the language that I have suggested.

My point here is that you will need help after reading this book: some help with motivation, some with sharing your experience and some with accountability. I would strongly urge you to get a buddy to work with on this, organizing a weekly meeting or a call. This only needs to take 15 minutes, running through which referrals are coming up and testing each other on the preparation.

In these calls, you should ask your buddy what their bridge line will be (explained in Chapter 6), remind them to ask for one name only, test them on the qualifying criteria, and then run through the follow-up process.

Ask which referrals are outstanding and whether the follow-up is being done. (This methodology is covered in later chapters in the book.)

Then look at each other's lists and confirm that everything on them is being taken care of. Get into the habit of doing this and you will really see the culmination of this book's advice in practice. I am certain that you will be rewarded.

Be bold and more ambitious

What I see from training and working with people is that predominantly we don't think boldly or ambitiously enough. As a result, we end up thinking that we don't deserve to build a big business, or that being comfortable and not stretched is enough. My advice here is to be bold, think big and ask big. Be brave in your referral question, asking for the biggest kind of client that you can possibly achieve.

Remember, the milestone for 'what is reasonable' is not 'what seems familiar to you', but rather 'what is reasonable to the person you are talking with'.

Holding the hand of the client who has made the referral

Once you have been given a referral:

- How do you make the client feel comfortable about the process?
- How do you keep your client informed about the progression of the referral from prospect to client?
- How do you ensure that your client has any information, including uncomfortable information, which is important for them to have during the process when you are working with them to become a client (sometimes called the on-boarding process); and also once their friend, colleague or contact has become a client?

For example, sometimes a first meeting arranged via a referral might lead to nothing and, of course, that is fine. I would suggest saying to the client: 'Thank you. In the end, I will not be working with the person you referred me to, but it was great to meet them.' This rounds the circle, leaving a client who has made a referral with a good feeling; this will make them more amenable to being asked for another referral further down the road.

However, there might also have been something that this prospect was unhappy with during the pitching or on-boarding process. You may wonder if the client and the friend or colleague/contact they introduced will be speaking negatively about you and the firm. Therefore, it is good etiquette to bring up with the client how you normally deal with information relating to the person they have referred you to, naturally always acknowledging confidentiality.

Chapter 4:

Summary Points

Make it easier for yourself

- Give clients better service and contact. Ensure hand-holding in difficult times. Follow up effectively and be aware of bringing the right resources of the firm to your client.
- Empower yourself. Turn negativity in your mind to positivity around referrals.
- Be aware of the positive language changes you use in meetings where you ask for referrals. Repeat them and note them down.
- Appreciate and be passionate about the values and USPs you offer clients.
- Organize your time better.
- Get a buddy system working around referral support.
- Who will you ask to buddy with you? Can you start this next week?
- Be bold and more ambitious. You may think you already have challenging targets. Increase them by 20% and ask yourself how you can achieve that. If you were convinced that referrals would help you achieve these targets, would that make it easier for you to ask for referrals?
- Discuss with your client how to keep them up to date about their referred friend/colleague/ contact, always respecting confidentiality.

Chapter 5

Improving Your Confidence

The body language we use when asking for referrals can be an overlooked subject. But it is crucial – as American essayist Ralph Waldo Emerson said: 'What you do speaks so loud that I cannot hear what you say.'[5] We speak how we speak, sit how we sit and ask how we ask. There are a few subtle points to make here. When we are asking for a referral, it is important not to ask in a way that suggests desperation or a lack of belief in what we are asking for. The advice offered on body language in this chapter seeks to address an important part of our preparation.

We will review quick wins to improve your confidence, whether through non-verbal communication, such as body language, or by eliminating words that make you come across as lacking confidence. We will also look at how to rephrase what you say to increase its impact.

First, you need to feel confident. It is essential that you also look confident. This is somewhat 'chicken and egg': when you feel confident, you look confident. Conversely, when you look and act more confident, you will feel more confident. This is important because when you are asking for a referral, you want to give your client the impression that you have asked many times before and the outcome is not crucial for you. A client may say 'no'. However, if they do, that will be due to any number of reasons that are

---

[5] Available at: www.google.co.uk/amp/s/quoteinvestigator.com/2011/01/27/what-you-do-speaks/amp/

completely unrelated to you and your firm. It might be a bad previous experience, with a person they referred someone to not following it up with the utmost professionalism. It could just be a client remaining extremely private about their affairs. The reason does not really matter and is not necessarily about you. The way that you ask suggests confidence and nonchalance as to the outcome. Ironically, this increases the probability of a positive outcome by removing one cause of a negative one: the needy request.

Often in my training, I urge participants in role-play to examine phrases where weakening words such as 'maybe' or 'possibly' crop up:

- 'Maybe you might know someone?'
- 'Maybe, when you get the chance, you could give them a call to introduce me.'
- 'Maybe you could get back to me to let me know when you have asked.'
- 'Do you possibly know one person?'
- 'I wonder if you could possibly help me?'

There is no need to use 'maybe' or 'possibly' as they weaken your message, so let's avoid these sorts of words. Let's see the same examples without using them:

- Do you know one person?
- When you get the chance, could you give them a call to introduce me?
- If you could get back to me to let me know when you have asked, that would be great.
- I wonder if you could help me?

When we ask, it is also important to sit up with a confident posture and speak slowly in a measured manner with credibility and assurance. This will help your client or contact to not even ask for one moment whether you might let them down or disappoint the person they put you in touch with. Posture indicates confidence levels. Sitting up straight with our shoulders back, making us vulnerable, shows we do not fear the situation. Bending forward shows we are afraid and seeking to protect ourselves. Would you rather make a referral for someone displaying confidence or for someone indicating fear?

Lowering stress

How do you help people to naturally fall into the best body language? There are two ways I recommend. The first is to approach a meeting where you plan to ask for a referral from a business point of view only. We are affected psychologically by our past and by our fears of rejection and this all leads to not asking or procrastination. So, before you go into any meeting, take some really deep breaths and let out the fear very slowly as you exhale. By breathing deeply, you are tricking your body into thinking that there is no danger. You are therefore less likely to display the typical fight–flight–freeze–fawn response to danger, all of which reduce your ability to manage the meeting effectively. If you take three deep breaths before you go into a meeting it will help.

A second way is to smile broadly and breathe at the same time, realizing on each breath that you are smiling. This changes the normal thought processes going through your mind. Changing yourself physiologically will change how you feel. The normal patterns of thinking you go into will be halted and you will be able to go into the meeting with a different perspective. Believe it or not, this is rooted in science. When psychologist Paul Ekman studied[6] how the

---

[6] Available at: www.paulekman.com/resources

emotions we feel are displayed as microexpressions, he also observed something unexpected. When he would re-create the muscle contractions on his face, he started feeling the corresponding emotion. By smiling, we can trick our body into feeling more positive. If this does not come naturally to you, you can simply place a pen across your mouth. This will activate the appropriate muscles and put you in a more positive mindset.

This can also be achieved by doing five star jumps before you go into a meeting or by grabbing your ear. There are many things you can do, so find one that works for you. In the meeting, if you feel fear coming on, or as people often say to me, you are 'about to ask but then don't', it can be useful to take a breath discreetly at this moment, breathing slowly as you are now in front of a client. As your stress levels drop, you will regain control and increase the probability of being comfortable with asking.

Or you could try a few techniques in the meeting that take you out of your head.

- Try breathing and follow your breath.
- Count your breath three times.
- Notice the toes on your feet or the fingers on your hand.
- Smile and make an effort to notice your smile.

These will all help, but it is best to do the one that works for you. Find something that helps to ground you in the present moment and ignore the fear of a negative outcome. Remember, if you get a 'no', all you will have lost is hope and you will gain capacity for chasing after another referral. The worst outcome of asking for a referral isn't a 'no'; it is getting a referral that demands your time and leads nowhere.

When you actually ask for the referral, look your client in the eye and keep focused on him or her. I know that we have all heard this before, but if you do look elsewhere when you are asking something, you lose a powerful effect. An element of disbelief enters the equation; something that tells the client that you don't mean what you are saying 100% or that there is something you don't believe in.

This is all happening in the subconscious for your client, but you don't want them to have any of their own triggers going off that somehow prevent them from being super-positive and helpful to you in finding a referral.

The actual words you use are also important to portray the confidence which shows that you have asked for referrals many times before and it does not really matter what response you get. The fact is, that if you do get a referral, you will really look after this person.

Chapter 5:

Summary Points

Improving your confidence

- Omit 'maybe' or 'possibly' when asking for a referral in a meeting.
- Assume a confident, upright seated posture.
- Don't let your eyes wander when asking for a referral.
- Use breathing and other techniques to reduce anxiety and get in the right zone before going into a meeting.

Ask colleagues to give you feedback after a meeting on how you present, your posture and if you looked the person in the eye when you asked for a referral.

Part Two

How to Ask for Referrals: A 7-Step Plan

7 Steps to Asking for Referrals

7 Follow up effectively

6 Prepare your client

5 Listen to the client's response

4 Qualify the referral

3 Ask for only one name

2 Find a bridge line

1 Homework

Chapter 6

Preparing to Ask
(Steps 1 and 2)

The importance of groundwork was succinctly expressed by US statesman Benjamin Franklin: 'By failing to prepare, you are preparing to fail.'[7] The whole point about asking for a referral in a meeting is that you are not just winging it and randomly asking. 'Preparing to ask' is therefore the first stage of our 7-step plan for mastering asking for referrals. This stage is about planning when to ask and what you will say. I am not sure how you plan or choreograph a meeting, but I always like to know how much time I have for a meeting, exactly how I will use the time, who will be there, what the dynamics are going to be, what questions I am going to ask and what I want the outcome to be.

Let's assume it's a meeting between you and a client and that you have an hour. The meeting's formal focus, whether it is the introduction of a new product or part of your business needing a review, has already been pre-agreed. Plan how you will use the various parts of the meeting and when you plan to bring up asking for a referral.

Step 1: Homework

By preparation for the referral, I am asking you to think about getting the perfect referral. That means asking yourself

---

[7] Available at: www.google.co.uk/amp/s/www.businessinsider.com/ 7-must-read-life-lessons-from-benjamin-franklin-2011-7%3famp

whether your client has mentioned a person or a company that you always thought it would be great to have as a client. Was he or she talking about a friend, family member, former colleague, board director or trustee of a charity they know? Of course, it is perfect if the name comes up naturally in conversation at the meeting.

The other part of the preparation is to try and think for this particular client. How could you find out who, among their contacts, would be a perfect referral for you? Do you need to look into their company at board level or at the other boards your client sits on? Can you find their contacts listed at the charities that your client is involved in? Think about what the client has told you at previous meetings about strong senior-level contacts they have in other companies. Try to think laterally and smartly; this is not something that should take longer than 10 minutes. Don't worry about whether the client might think that you have been studying them if your prepa-ration gives you away. Today's world is extremely open, and knowing who somebody is likely to know is merely good business as well as a matter of human interest. Your client is not likely to find it at all disconcerting that you have found a link to someone they know. In all likelihood, they are well used to being asked 'Do you know person A?'.

I know it can be tempting to wing it, improvise, 'play it by ear' and hope all will go well. But decades of experi-ence have convinced me that a little thoughtful preparation goes a long way. Apparently, Steve Jobs, one of the master presenters, would rehearse each presentation three times. 'But given his role and audience, that makes sense. My case is different,' you might say. Yes, indeed. However, what is at stake in your meeting? If you win the referral, how much is it really worth to you? A few thousand pounds of revenue per year? How much is that worth over the average lifetime of a relationship? Remember, we are talking of investing a few minutes in preparing. It is easy to find excuses to avoid this. However, my goal is to give you a roadmap of key points that will make a significant difference, so it is easier to find the time and significantly increase your likelihood of success.

I would suggest scheduling a few minutes in your calendar for this step before each meeting, maybe even a few days before. When we make an appointment with ourselves, it is easier to respect this appointment. Try to avoid scheduling it right before the meeting, as you run the risk of skipping it altogether.

Step 2: Find your bridge line

The second step in the 7-step plan, another part of your preparations ahead of the meeting, is 'finding your bridge line'. You must think about what bridge line to use to introduce the request for a referral. I will assume that now you have planned the meeting, you know how long it will last. I always advise people not to leave a referral request until the end of a meeting, because this can feel like you are taking something from the client. It can also feel 'salesy' to bring it up as you are gathering your papers to leave a meeting, rather than asking at a moment that is very appropriate.

There are a number of good moments to bring up the bridge line:

a. It can be initiated by 'asking for feedback'

This can usefully set up a bridge line to asking for a referral. It is best to frame the asking for feedback widely, something like: 'Rachel, we have worked together for a number of years. It would be great to get a sense of how you view the relationship over the years we have worked together, more specifically the product, services and the levels of trust.'

This wide frame prevents a client from speaking in a concentrated manner on one aspect that has been frustrating them in the short term, and you are drawing them to think of the relationship as a whole over a much longer period. It is also advisable to pick clients where you are pretty certain that the feedback will be positive. Of course, it is a competitive world and these clients will be approached by your competitors, so sometimes people are afraid of inviting negativity. However, if there are any negative feelings, this is a fine opportunity to hear and confront them. And remember that not addressing them does not make them go away; it just means they have room to grow and you will reduce your ability to address more or less legitimate concerns.

If you have asked for the feedback, I would suggest timing this for the first part of the meeting. Then in the last 10 minutes, where you would normally address any other business (AOB), having heard the response to your question on feedback, you can say as a bridge line: 'That was very interesting, the feedback you gave me earlier in the meeting on our relationship. I agree with it and it leads me to ask you for your help on one thing.'

b. Take advantage of a client asking how your business is going

Your client might talk about their company, the business of a friend or the state of the economy; this gives you a perfect segue to acknowledge this and ask some questions that lead naturally into talking about your firm, the developments in your division or what your business is now specifically focusing on. You might say, for example: 'Over the last year, we have continued to build our business and have created more capacity and we are looking now to expand our focus.'

Then, once again in the AOB, you can refer to having discussed the business and drop into the conversation that its strategy has led to some spare capacity. You might say: 'As you know, at least half of our business is brought in by referrals, and now, as I mentioned earlier, we have some spare capacity. I would love to ask for your help on one thing.'

Or, if the client was brought in by a referral: 'As you were introduced by Mr X, you know that our business is built on referrals. We would love to find more people like you/more businesses like yours that we can work with. I would love to ask for your help on one thing.'

c. A bridge line can be stated as values or USPs of your firm that will resonate with the client

These will be values that keep the client tied to your firm. The common denominator values which are important are trust and service.

A list could also include those from Chapter 4's section on values and USPs, or from the following:

- defining a strategy
- connecting deeply with your clients, and finding out about their aspirations, motivations and plan in life
- obsession with client focus
- the collegiate atmosphere within your firm
- outward corporate values
- internal values that show your company is different to the marketplace
- the speed of your feedback to clients
- efficient service
- entrepreneurial aspects of your firm

- planning advice
- products you have found for the client recently
- helpful education about your products and services
- excellent reporting.

In the AOB part of the meeting, you can say something like:

- 'I know you have appreciated the following values/ USPs of our firm being X, Y or Z ...'
- 'I know you have appreciated the clarity and structure we have set up for you over the last couple of years and you have found it very valuable.'
- 'You brought up in the meeting how you appreciated our focus and service.'
- 'I am happy to see that as a client of our firm you have experienced peace of mind, being able to use us as a sounding board, and help in making important decisions.'

After one of these lines, you can add: 'This leads me to ask for your help on one thing.'

d. The bridge line can refer to a former business colleague who previously managed this client but has now left the firm

'I know you have been a client of X for a number of years, and from speaking to Fatima, who worked with you for many years, that you appreciate the following values of the firm (use the appropriate values from the above list) ... I would love to ask for your help on one thing ...'

Or, if you have transitioned to a new company with your client, you could say: 'Obviously, I am very happy with how this transition has gone and how we have settled

into this new firm, and it would be great to get some feedback on the change … Also, I'd love to ask for your help
on one thing.'

e. A bridge line can use the history of the relationship

Here I use an example related to wealth management. You
can substitute what the main aims of your client were 'x'
number of years ago.

'We have been working together for x years, and when
we first met, your main aims were to (use one or more of the
following):

- consolidate your portfolios
- diversify your wealth
- plan for your children and retirement
- have a sounding board
- create a balance in life between your investments,
  company and the personal family future
- create a selection of portfolios with certain risk
  parameters

… and I am happy to say we have achieved it and, on the
way, got to know each other well. This leads me to ask for
your help on one thing …'

f. You can develop a bridge line around providing a schedule to the client of what will be covered in the meeting

On such a schedule, you can write 'referral request' or
'exploring the opportunity of a referral'. This option clearly

warms up a client for the areas you will be covering in the meeting and alerts him or her to the referral question.

g. You can develop a bridge line by leveraging a friendship

Each client is different, with a distinct background and length and depth of relationship with you. Some may have become friends or absolutely love your products and service, so you can be more up front and direct with them. You could say:

- 'Andrei, we have a great relationship, and I know you would be willing to help me.'
- 'Hiroshi, you know me well and you know how effective our products and services are. I'd like to ask for your help on one thing.'

WORKSHEET

The pre-planned name and the bridge line

Please look at your client list again. Think laterally about previous meetings or spend some time conducting some searches around your client and add one name that you know a particular client is connected to, who would make a perfect referral. Please add it to the following worksheet.

Also add to the worksheet the bridge line you would choose to use for this particular client.

Client name	Contact of client who has come up in previous meeting or with research	Most appropriate bridge line

Exercise

Take your last two meetings; think about their content, how the meetings went and what was said. Try to think what would have been the most appropriate bridge line to have used from the list above.

What was said in that meeting specific to the values or USPs that you experienced during the client relationship?

Was there a natural moment when the conversation mentioned how well the relationship is going? Could this have been a moment to have asked for further feedback?

Did they ask you how the business was going? Or did they talk about their business?

Was there a schedule you brought to that meeting which you could have used?

Becoming aware of the opportunities we missed makes it easier to seize them the next time they present themselves.

Chapter 6:

Summary Points

Preparing to ask

Step 1: Homework

- **Has your client ever mentioned a contact that in your mind would make the perfect referral opportunity for you?**

Step 2: Find your bridge line

- **Ask for multifaceted feedback on the relationship.**
- **Describe how your business is going and explain you have now increased capacity.**
- **Describe the values and USPs of your firm that your client has experienced with you.**
- **Detail the history of the relationship: the initial aims of the relationship and how you have delivered.**
- **Use a schedule for the meeting to make your client aware you will bring up a referral request in the meeting.**
- **Leverage a strong friendship that has developed with your client.**

Chapter 7

Leading the Conversation (Steps 3, 4 and 5)

The leading industrialist and philanthropist Andrew Carnegie memorably said: 'If you want to be happy, set a goal that commands your thoughts, liberates your energy and inspires your hopes.'[8] If you know there is a person whom a client knows well who would make a perfect referral for you, you can use one of the bridge line examples set out in Chapter 6, followed by:

- 'Dénes, I know you have appreciated the trust and the services of our business over the last couple of years and have found the relationship very valuable. That leads me to ask for your help on one thing. You have talked in the past about Mrs X. I believe she would make a great referral. Could I ask you to make an introduction for me, please?'
- 'Dénes, I know you have appreciated ... I have noticed that Mr X is in your association/your club/on your board/in your team/involved in the charity you support. He'd make a great referral. Could I ask you to make an introduction for me please?'

---

[8] Available at: https://quotefancy.com/quote/758250/Andrew-Carnegie-If-you-want-to-be-happy-set-a-goal-that-commands-your-thoughts-liberates

Prepare for a possible refusal

At this point, the answer may be: 'You know, Graham, I would love to help you, but for personal reasons I would prefer not to introduce you.'

What is important here is that you do not regard this as fobbing you off. There can be many reasons why it may not be suitable for a client to give you a referral to this particular contact at this point in time.

If it is a business partner, they may not want to mix business with pleasure.

Or there might be an uncomfortable link to this person for personal reasons, so they prefer not to go there.

However, it gives you the opportunity to respond: 'I absolutely understand and appreciate where you are coming from.'

Then you fall back upon the process outlined below – asking for one other person that they know.

Step 3: Ask for only one name

The third step of our 7-step plan for how to ask for business referrals involves you only asking for one name, one referral from your client. A common mistake is to ask: '… if there is anyone you know or any friends or business colleagues that you would be happy to introduce to me.'

In all my experience, I feel this is too much to ask. A client finds it difficult to focus their mind and to think of one name at that moment if the question is too general. To ensure you have the best opportunity to get a referral name brought up at that meeting, say instead:

- 'Sven, I'd love to ask for your help on one thing. Is there one person with whom you have a strong connection who you would be happy to refer me to?'

- 'Nabila, I'd love to explore something with you. Is there one contact with whom you have a strong connection who you would be happy to introduce me to?'
- 'Bertrand, I'd love to brainstorm something with you. Is there one business contact at the equivalent senior position to yourself, with whom you have a strong connection, who you would be able to introduce me to?'
- 'Miriam, I'd love to ask you a favour. Is there one company, with whom you have a strong connection, which you would be happy to refer me to?'

***

Here are some other wording variables illustrating the point with examples for a wealth manager:

- 'Is there one person you know?'
- 'Is there one family that you know?'
- 'Is there one person you know in your neighbourhood (if you know it is likely that there is one)?'
- 'Is there one person you know at a senior level in your company?'
- 'Is there one person you know on the board of your company?'
- 'Is there one person you know on the board of X charity?'

Step 4: Qualify the referral

The fourth step in our 7-step plan for asking for referrals involves qualifying exactly what you are looking for in terms of the type of client you want to be referred to. This stage is of the utmost importance. You are busy and time management is really important. Therefore, you need to use the opportunity well and be bold and brave. Naturally, we assume that, because a client knows us and our products and services, they would surely know who to introduce to us. This is actually not the case. A client would not know the perfect referral for you.

Let's all be honest. Who hasn't received a referral that turned out to be a bit of a dud and then took a lot of time to follow up? I am guessing that most of you have had this experience. Once the referral was given, you did not want to let down your client or cause offence so you met the person they referred you to but quickly realized it wasn't a good use of your time. Then there was an uncomfortable situation – having to tell the person to whom you were referred that this business relationship is not the right fit for your company. And all this, of course, made it harder with the client who gave you the referral. You could ask them again, but you have probably wasted some goodwill.

How to qualify your referral?

To help you make this decision, look at your top 10 clients for a few minutes and ask yourself some of the following questions to confirm who the best 10 clients are and what you would like to look for in a new client. Are they:

- clients you really enjoy working with, whether by location, age or character?
- clients with whom you have a strong working relationship?
- profitable clients, with short- and long-term potential?
- clients who really value and appreciate the service you offer?

- clients who are less demanding or less time-consuming?

Now spend some time denoting your least-preferred clients and run through a similar exercise to the above, working out why they are less preferred. The results should inform you of the type of client you are looking for and which type you are looking to avoid. Use some of this information when you qualify, as exactly as you can, what sort of individual you would like a client to refer to you.

***

I will first illustrate some helpful lines for a wealth management client. These will help focus the mind of a client on a candidate with the right financial assets. You are asking: ' Is there one person …'

- 'in a similar financial position or situation to you?'
- 'with a similar financial wealth and complexity to you?'
- 'with similar needs and requirements that we can help with?'
- 'in a similar network as you?'
- 'with a similarly sized portfolio as yours?'
- 'with similar characteristics to you, such as X? I would love to look after more people like you. We provide a bespoke service so cannot deal with just anyone.'
- 'who has created a portfolio similar to the one you started?'
- 'who thinks about our firm the same way as you do?'
- 'with a similar financial sophistication?'

If the client is a company, you are asking: 'Is there one company ...'

- 'in a similar situation to your company?
- 'with similar needs and requirements that we can help with?'
- 'with similar characteristics to your company, such as X?'
- 'that sees our firm through the same eyes as you?'

Here is a full example, including steps 2, 3 and 4 of our 7-step plan:

- Step 2: 'I know you've appreciated our excellent reporting, obsession with client focus, planning advice and overall relationship over the years we've worked together. I'd love to ask for your help on one thing.'
- Step 3: 'Is there one family you have a strong connection with who you'd be happy to introduce me to?'
- Step 4: 'Being more specific, is there a family that might need management of a portfolio of a similar size and sophistication to yours, and see our firm in the same light that you do? I'm asking a select number of clients, with whom I have a particularly strong connection.'

Or you can phrase it as follows if the client is a company:

- Step 2: 'I know you've appreciated the excellent breadth of our products and services and our overall relationship over the years we've worked together. I'd love to ask for your help on one thing.'

- Step 3: 'Is there one person in a similar position to you at another company with whom you have a strong connection that you'd be happy to introduce me to?'
- Step 4: 'Being more specific, is there a company that might have a need for products and services similar to those we offer, and sees our firm the same way as you do? I'm asking a select number of clients, with whom I have a particularly strong connection.'

Here you will notice I have used a bridge line using values and USPs. Of course, as explained already, there are multiple permutations – using different bridge lines and following with different qualifying lines.

Step 5: Listening to the client's response

The importance of listening was stressed by the novelist Ernest Hemingway: 'I like to listen. I have learned a great deal from listening carefully. Most people never listen.'[9]

Even though you might not be a natural salesperson, you will definitely have heard that the role of a good salesperson is to be a good listener. In this instance, your role at this moment, after asking for the referral, is to listen to what the client has to say. Step 5 of our 7-step plan for asking for a referral involves listening very carefully to the client's response.

---

[9] Available at: https://www.goodreads.com/quotes/353013-i-like-to-listen-i-have-learned-a-great-deal

Normally it comes down to one of three responses:

1. **'Graham, I would love to help you. Let me have a think about who I could introduce to you.'**
    When responding to this line from your client, it is very important you have the positive and right mindset, because this response from your client is not negative and is not a rejection. So, the reply to this is important to set up the opportunity to re-ask naturally and not feel uncomfortable or even slightly embarrassed.

    You might respond: 'Yes, absolutely. That would be great, I need to get back to you from this meeting with X and Y in the next week or so. Do you mind if I ask you then if you've had a chance to think of one introduction?'

    Now that you have teed up an opportunity to ask this client again, you must ask within one week to 10 days and remember they are not fobbing you off or being negative. It is in your own head if you think they are. So, when you ask within 10 days, probably over the phone, you can do so with confidence: 'Mei, you mentioned in the meeting a week ago that you would try and think of one person to introduce me to. Did one come to mind?'

2. **'I would love to help you, Graham, but all my strong contacts in companies are covered in this area.'**
    This line can feel like a blow and a shutdown – a clear signal that this person is not interested. However, if we question how true it is, we know so many private reasons why someone may be absolutely at the place of needing to speak to you. These reasons may not

be known by your client. It may be that their contact has come into some money to invest; or the person is unhappy with his current service and would really appreciate a second opinion on the diversification of assets. For those of you who might be seeking referral to a company, it may be that this company is unhappy with their current service and would really appreciate a second opinion in terms of approach and methodology.

Therefore, you can answer: 'It's excellent that they've been covered over the years, but there might be some things they've missed. A sense check or second point of view is always useful and of course they might be looking to diversify, or could be unhappy. So, is there one contact who you think might benefit from a chat? If that leads to nothing, then don't worry. I appreciate your thinking on this.'

3. 'Well, yes. Actually, I can think of someone.'
It is really important to ask there and then who they are thinking of. You might think this is obvious, but I have heard hundreds of times about salespeople who did not take this opportunity and just left it without saying: 'Great. Do you mind if I ask who you are thinking of?'

At this point, you have the opportunity to make the short meeting you will have with the person they refer you to, slightly warmer as you will know a little more about this person.

Here are a few questions you could ask – just to get a sense of how your client knows them, whether it is through work, a charity or a business they have worked with or through a friend or neighbour.

- • 'That is great. Out of interest, was there something specific that caused you to think of X?'
- • 'Is there anything specific you think it would be good for me to know ahead of a short meeting with Mr X?'

This opens up the possibility for your client to give you some information about the person they are referring you to and, of course, that will help you assess if this person will be a good referral.

Chapter 7:

Summary Points

Leading the conversation

Step 3: Ask for only one name

- **Ask for a referral to a person your client knows and has talked about.**
- **If a referral to this person is not possible, ask for ONE other person.**
- **Only ask for ONE name when asking for a referral. Listen to what you ask for in next client meetings you have. Are you asking for ONE name only? If not, please try it and practise it. You will notice the difference it makes to success.**

Step 4: Qualify the referral

- **Be brave. Qualify precisely the sort of referral you are looking for to ensure you get the near perfect introduction. Try the next time to qualify precisely and listen to how it feels doing it this way. Notice how much clearer it is to ask the client for exactly what you want and the different sort of response your client gives.**

Step 5: Listening to the client's response

- **Listen intently to the client's response to your request. Who are they referring you to? If they cannot think of someone immediately, ask if you can get back to them in a week.**
- **If they said they could think of someone, did you ask them there and then who they were thinking of?**

Chapter 8

Preparing Your Client
(Step 6)

According to the management consultant and educator Peter Drucker, 'Strategy is a commodity, execution is an art.'[10]

'Preparing your client' is the sixth step in our 7-step plan for asking for referrals. Here we need to address why a referral actually works. The most important quality at this stage is trust. After that, it is about the client being well looked after, receiving good service and prospering over the long term.

Clearly, this is where a referral breaks through. When we respect people, we give weight and credibility to what they say about other people. There is proof of this in your life. It is very evident when you give or make referrals yourself. How your referrer talks or writes about you to their friend or business contact is extremely important.

Imagine the different chances of success in obtaining a referral if the following different sentences are used:

- 'Ludmila, you should meet Jacques.'
- 'Kevin, Chichima is a very bright person. You should speak to her about her work.'
- 'Camila, I am a client of Vasilios. You should meet him.'

---

[10] Available at: www.strategyandcomplexity.guide/quotes/strategy-is-a-commodity-execution-is-an-art-2/

Or:

- 'Sayora, I have been working with Richard and his firm for the last two years. I trust him and the service given to me over the years has been invaluable, I recommend you have a quick coffee/video conference with him.'
- 'Margaux, I want to suggest you have a coffee/ video conference with Katerina from X firm. I have been a client of Katerina's for five years, I trust her completely and her firm has delivered on what we set out to achieve together from the outset. I feel very confident to recommend Katerina and X firm.'

Your prospect is already 50% sold by the fact that you have been referred by someone they trust implicitly.

All this means that what your client says to the person he or she is referring you to is incredibly important. The prospect you are being referred to needs to feel that it is an absolute no-brainer that they should meet you. Even if they have no immediate need, they know that meeting you for a short time will be interesting and insightful and they will learn something new.

The most powerful thing to say to your client at this point is:

- 'What has worked very well for me in the past is …'
- 'What would be very powerful for me is …'
- 'What I have seen from past experience and would be most helpful for me right now is …'

And then add: 'If you could call X for a quick chat first, to introduce me and explain how we have worked together and the trust and quality of relationship we enjoy, this would be really appreciated.'

***

You will know the firm's values and the USPs that have benefited your client and will resonate with him or her. Remind the client of these, as it will be very convincing and authentic if he or she repeats these values and USPs to the prospect.

- 'It would be really appreciated if you could call X for a quick chat first, to introduce me and explain that you have received excellent trust, service and advice as a client and would highly recommend me and my firm.'
- 'I would be very grateful if you could call X for a quick chat first, to introduce me and explain some of the elements of our working relationship that you have experienced – for example, how we connect deeply with our clients and find out about their aspirations and motivations. It would be really appreciated if you would highly recommend me and my firm.'

Your client will either be happy to make a phone call, as discussed above, or they will prefer to send an email introducing and recommending you. Either way, once this has been done, you need to ensure they send a three-way email that makes the connection and sets you up to speak. Now you can follow up.

What's important here is to do it quickly – ideally on the same day as the three-way email was sent. Normally I suggest waiting a few hours, so that you do not look too keen.

I then suggest thanking your client for the introduction and adding that you will write separately to the person you are being referred to. Then, on a separate email sent only to the referred prospect, suggest a quick meeting over a coffee and ask when they might be free.

Using the word 'quick' takes the pressure off. It also does not suggest any form of desperation.

Alternatively, after thanking your client, write a separate direct email to the prospect asking for a two-minute phone conversation. Ask them to suggest a date and time that suit, adding that you will call in a few days if you have not heard from them.

Limiting the call to two minutes at this point, even if it ends up being longer, makes it psychologically much easier for the prospect to agree to chat. You are also making it easier for you to follow up if they don't reply. This is polite but not pushy and ensures that you will have the chance to take things further.

Clearly, this is much less important for the prospect than it is for you and you should not therefore take it personally if they do not reply. Just assume they have important things going on in their life at this time. But it is also reasonable to follow up personally.

Saying that you will call in the next few days of course assumes that you have their work telephone number. If not, call your client and ask for the contact details.

If there is no answer when you call the prospect, it is not a good idea to leave your name or a message on this first occasion. Try again two days later but again don't leave your name on any voicemail. If you try a third time, leave a message: 'Hi John, my name is Lenka Burstall. I am following up the introduction by Wayne Thomas, I'll try and catch you again next week.'

If a prospect has indicated to your client that he or she is happy to be connected with you, remember that they still want to be helped. You therefore need to counter your natural thought that the lack of communication represents a rejection.

Holding feet to the fire

Once you have asked for a referral, you have done the hard work, or most of it. But what people say and do in a meeting is different to what they might do when they have left the room. This is in no way a reflection of you. Your client might just forget to make the referral. In this case, here are some ways of making it easy to get back to your client.

This is what I suggest you say in the meeting: 'If I have not seen a three-way email in the next week or so, do you mind if I give you a little nudge to remind you to make the referral? I know how busy you can get.'

This is important. If you don't say anything, it is much harder to raise the subject again and your mind will tell you to just leave it and move on. Letting your client know removes any confusion about the situation.

What not to do at this vital point

1. *DO NOT ask for the phone number of the prospect or try to call them without a referral having been made.*
   It may seem straightforward to call them, mentioning your client's name. But it considerably weakens your chance of success with the prospect. The transition of trust does not happen if the client does not handle it personally. In my experience, taking this action weakens this element of trust by 50%. If you ring the

prospect out of the blue, you also move into slight hassling mode. And you may weaken trust in another way too, as your prospect may not believe you when you say that the client told you to get in touch and mention their name. In my experience, doing this significantly lessens the odds of being able to arrange a meeting. There may also be some frustration from the referred prospect towards your client for setting up a referral in this way. Anything like this only acts to create a small negative regarding future referral requests to this client. If the client offers simply to provide you with the prospect's name and number, you could explain that many people value it when their friends act as gatekeepers. Even if the prospect would be okay with receiving a cold call, most people appreciate being asked first to give them the opportunity to decline without appearing rude.

2. *DO NOT ask the client to set up a drink with all three of you.*
    Again, this might seem a good plan. It sets up the trust well and clearly shows that your client wants to introduce you, trusts you and your firm and likes you. However, the prospect will not necessarily open up with your client present as he or she would in a one-on-one first meeting with you. Adopting this strategy might also make it a bit awkward to ensure that the next meeting is one-on-one with the prospect, which of course is what you really want.
    If this situation becomes unavoidable, I would suggest that you seize the opportunity of being alone with the prospect for a few moments when your client visits the bathroom or gets his/her coat. In this brief moment, suggest that the two of you meet again

over a coffee. Ask when it might suit them and try to confirm where the meeting will be.

3. *TRY TO AVOID the client arranging for the three of you to go together to a sporting event, to play a game of golf, to attend a musical event or an art show, etc.*

   This is another scenario where the all-important first meeting with your prospect is out of your control. Your client may just see it as a social event and not talk about you and your product or service at all. He or she may not have the opportunity to do so, or may be entertaining other people. Either way, it does not matter. At some point at the event, you need to find a quiet moment to say something like this: 'Ulrike, really good to meet you today, I know that Frederik mentioned that I work with him, it is a close relationship and I know he has appreciated how we have worked together.

   Now is clearly not the time, but let's meet for a brief coffee some time over the next two weeks at your office or nearby. What day suits you?'

   Once you have done this, you can rejoin the evening's conversation, with nothing related to work or the connection to your client.

4. *BE WARY of your client organizing a dinner party or social evening and seating you next to your potential prospect.*

   If this becomes unavoidable, my approach would be not to talk business or share more than a few words about what you do. It is nevertheless an opportunity to get to know the prospect and their business, ask insightful questions and just be yourself. What you do for a living will of course crop up in the conversation.

The prospect might, for example, say: 'Yes, Lavinia suggested that we meet up. It would be great to hear a little about what you do.'

You might be tempted to use this as a way to turn this conversation into a first meeting, but I would not recommend this. Instead, use the ideas I gave earlier. If the prospect does attempt to lure you into talking about your work, just give him or her half a minute on what you do in a very non-'salesy' way, adding: 'I could obviously go into a lot of detail now, but let's discuss some of these business matters at another time, if you agree. How about a coffee this week or next?'

When they agree, try to get a date in the diary. Then, immediately revert to something social or about the event, instead of anything about your job or the planned meeting.

Important

Once you have received the referral or the person at the social event or dinner has said that it would be great to meet, it is important to follow up the next day. It will definitely make a difference. Doing so immediately has by far the most impact. The prospect will remember much more clearly who you are, what your client said about you and why they should meet you.

This may sound quite obvious, but you would be surprised how many people wait one or maybe two or three weeks to respond. They get busy, other things come up or maybe something important happens for one of their clients. It really does not matter. As we all know, this is procrastination.

It will take just a few minutes to follow up the referral that was set up for you by your client. Please do not weaken the opportunity for success by delaying this vital communication unnecessarily.

Chapter 8:

Summary Points

Step 6: Preparing your client

- Don't assume that the client will introduce you to the prospect in the best way to ensure that a referral meeting takes place.
- Manage this process directly to ensure your client knows the best language to use to approach the referral with their friend or colleague.
  This step is key to success and needs practice, as it will feel counter-intuitive to be trying to push or direct your client on HOW to ask their contact to meet you.
- One of the lines to use to initiate this: 'What has worked for me in the past is … if you could …'
- Ask permission to give the client a nudge if you have not heard anything from them in a week or 10 days.
- Do not ask for the phone number of the prospect before obtaining a referral from the client.
- Do not push for the client to set up an introductory meeting with all three of you. The most powerful method is a one-on-one meeting with the prospect.

Chapter 9

Following Up Effectively (Step 7)

Sales writer Michelle Moore said memorably: 'Not following up with your clients is the same as filling up your bathtub without first putting the stopper in the drain.'[11]

'Following up effectively' is the final stage of our 7-step plan for successfully obtaining a referral. This is where I would say 30% of all attempts to ask for referrals fail. You have done most of the hard work, thought about your client, asked really well and you have your client wanting to help you. But at this point it is very easy for things to get in the way, so it is particularly important that you stay extremely focused.

This is one of the times when it is useful to have a buddy system with a colleague who helps you to stay on top and remain accountable. You will get busy and things will slip; it is natural. Once a week, have a five-minute chat or at least a check-in call with your buddy. Good luck and stay on top of it. Here are some pointers that will help.

Please fill out the following worksheet to monitor and follow up your referrals. This includes what the follow-up and plan of action with the client should be. It should include the moment when the client said they would make a call or send a three-way email. It also will have details of when the meeting with the prospect is going to take place.

---

[11] Available at: https://bukrate.com/author/michelle-moore

WORKSHEET

Monitor/follow up your referrals

Client who gave the referral	Name of prospect	How/when is the client getting in touch with the prospect?	Follow up with the client/plan of action

Download this worksheet and more resources at www.graham-eisner.com

Sometimes the client does not follow through and make contact with the person they referred you to

A client has offered to make the referral and committed to do it but forgets or gets distracted by other important issues. Weeks and months pass and nothing happens. Your mind tells you not to pester such a client. They said they'd do it, so something must have come up. They'll do it when they can. Unfortunately, this is not the case. You need to be on top of your clients in a friendly, non-pushy way. Remember, you already asked if they would mind being given a nudge if nothing happened. Whenever possible, call them in person: 'Erik, did you have a chance to call X? Can I ask you as a favour to make that call to X we talked about? Do you have a second today or tomorrow by any chance, please? Thanks.'

You might need to repeat this line two weeks later if you've still not heard from your client. Again, your mind will tell you to drop the matter. You will think that the client clearly doesn't really have the time or is unwilling to help and that it will only sound annoying if you ask again.

I would urge you to consider that it is absolutely worth trying again. You can remind the client that they happily agreed that you should give them a nudge in such an event. If you hear nothing back after three attempts, wait two months and try again.

Once your client has made the contact and copied you in on a three-way introductory email, follow up after a few hours, sending an email to the person to whom they referred you to arrange a short meeting. If days go by and the prospect still hasn't replied or called you, don't give up. Keep trying by phone. If you do not get any response from the prospect, keep trying to call once every two weeks. Only send an email once.

Many people ask me at what point they should just drop the effort and give up. I strongly suggest that they don't. If you use the tactics outlined above, you'll eventually speak directly to the prospect and you're likely to be very surprised. It'll be a friendly, easy conversation and they'll be very happy to meet. They'll be very polite and remember clearly what your client said to them. They'll show in their voice their willingness and need to meet you. You will also experience quite quickly an alleviation of your anxiety about this referral. You'll be glad you persevered and didn't give up. You followed through and experienced success.

Remember your success in getting the referral so you can use the strategy again

When we succeed in something, how we do that is often buried in our subconscious. However, by following this 7-step process to ask for referrals, you are using some new language and tools. Whether the secret of your success was subconscious or otherwise, I always suggest after a successful referral that you jot down, less than an hour after a meeting, answers to the questions below in a referral notebook:

- What made it work?
- What did you say that worked?
- What did the client respond well to?
- What was your bridge line?
- What was the language you used that worked?
- What ended up being the most powerful thing my client could do and actually did to ensure the referral?
- What would I use again in a meeting?
- How did I remind my client to make the call to person they referred me to?

- How did I feel once I got hold of person they referred me to and they were happy to meet?

It is important to write this down very soon after the referral meeting or after the call with the prospect. Otherwise, there is a good chance that you will forget what you actually did to earn your success.

Chapter 9:

Summary Points

Step 7: Following up effectively

- **About 30% of referrals don't happen because you failed to follow up your successful request to the client.**
- **You forget, you get too busy or become timid about reminding the client.**
- **Stay on top of your clients until they make the referral. They might forget or become too busy.**
- **If you do not get any response from the prospect, keep trying to call once every two weeks. Only send an email once.**

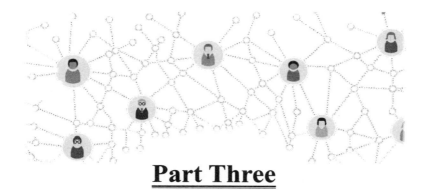

Part Three

Thinking Laterally

Chapter 10

Asking for Referrals from Intermediaries

The great British statesman Winston Churchill stressed that 'Success always demands a greater effort.'[12] Intermediary referrals deliver another valuable hidden pipeline of highly qualified prospects. Apart from client referrals, there are a variety of other very powerful sources to deliver referrals.

Intermediaries can include other companies targeting similar clients in a non-competitive way or other suppliers of complementary services.

You might think that normally this would involve providing an incentive in some form to these partners to receive a referral. However, this chapter will show you ways to create this relationship in such a way that it can deliver you a referral without you having to offer an incentive. You can help your intermediary and they can help you.

Who are these non-competitive partners in your case? Think laterally about this and brainstorm with others in your business or specific people outside it who could help you to identify these partners. Prioritize ones holding similar values to those of your company. You know that you can help them too.

In Chapters 11 and 12, I define intermediaries as including other potential introducers such as family, friends, former work colleagues or current colleagues.

---

[12] Available at: https://richardlangworth.com/success

In this chapter the majority of my examples are from the financial services industry. However, the methodology is directly transferable to whoever is the relevant intermediary for your business.

For a wealth manager, these intermediaries can include lawyers, accountants, trustees, family, friends, internal colleagues and also any professional entity that has similar high-net-worth clients such as yacht brokers, high-quality wine merchants and specialist real estate agents.

There are clearly great opportunities for receiving referrals from all the above, but in my experience very few people have a clear strategy for intermediaries.

Which of these types is truly worth prioritizing as a credible source of the referrals that you need to grow your business? Answering that question involves being deeply honest with yourself about your time management. So much time can be wasted establishing relationships that will not be fruitful or ones in which the partners are not upfront about trying to help each other and working out ways to do this.

Of course, apart from the lack of planning for a successful intermediary referral strategy, when we *are* working with good intermediaries, there are a number of mindsets that hold us back from asking for referrals:

- I don't know how to ask in a way that would be received well by the intermediary.
- An intermediary would give a referral if they had one, so there is no need to ask.
- An intermediary will only be interested if I offer a financial incentive in some form.
- This intermediary has nothing to gain from me or my business so why would they give me a referral?

- It would open up a 'Pandora's box' if I asked, as an intermediary might use it as a way to bring up something negative about the relationship.
- I have asked before and an intermediary said they would introduce someone, but it did not happen, so I don't feel confident about asking again.
- I have not known this intermediary long enough to ask.
- I asked an intermediary recently and don't want to ask them again.

With all these mindsets, you are assuming what the intermediary will be thinking and how they'll act. You're projecting how you think and your insecurities onto the intermediary. Fear is entering the equation and your mind is producing stories that persuade you not to ask and potentially go where it might be uncomfortable. The honest truth is that, just like many of the mindsets in Chapter 3, none of these thoughts should hold you back from asking. I've included most of the relevant mindsets relating to intermediaries, but there are also others on the list in Chapter 3 that will probably resonate for you. Please remember to read the reasons why these mindsets are not actually valid.

Of course, there are some nuances to take into account. If anything, asking intermediaries is easier than asking clients because they expect you to ask. But in your list of intermediaries, there will be people who have delivered some referrals in the last year or two and others who have not delivered any.

In this chapter, I would like to help you appreciate which of these intermediaries are worth keeping and worth nurturing. In all cases, I hope that you become very clear on how to take intermediary relationships to the next level and what can ensure that they will deliver referrals to you.

At the top of the worksheet, write the names of intermediaries who represent existing referrals for you. It should be the name of a solo operator or the name of the intermediary you have contact with within a company. Now, on the left-hand side you can see I have asked many questions and the aim here is for you to get a true sense of your intermediary relationships. I would like you to use 0–5 as a gauge, with 0 denoting the lowest score and 5 meaning excellent. The six questions also appear here with descriptions so you can see clearly how to rank 0–5.

1. **How good are they at delivering referrals?**
   This is where we need to be honest with ourselves. How long have you been spending on each intermediary and how many referrals have resulted over the last year? Is this up to expectations? Could they give you more? How would you rate them between 0–5, including the quality of the referrals received? We know there is competition for prospects from other firms, so where do we stand against our competitors in that regard? What is the likelihood they will give you more referrals in the future? Why might you believe they would? Have you discussed it with them or are you hoping they will?

   Of course, you want to be front of mind when a referral opportunity comes up. You will know what information has been given to intermediaries and whether it was given personally or as part of a group. If it is the latter, I would bet that this was not powerful enough. You had a nice meeting, presented your firm's credentials and received theirs, but what did that lead to? I would suggest strongly that you focus on a one-on-one meeting with a key intermediary decision-maker who can make a referral. If there are four people within an intermediary firm who can give referrals, I would arrange four different meetings (one with each of them) and create four separate relationships. They will think differently, have different egos and each will need to be treated differently and shown they are special to your firm in order for you to really understand what will lead them to give a referral and perhaps what has held them back in the past.

2. **How well does the intermediary understand your business, USPs and client characteristics?**
Do your intermediaries really understand what differentiates your firm from your competitors and what are your firm's true values and unique selling points? Do they fully appreciate the characteristics of the clients you look after, and why? Do they understand what constitutes a perfect client referral for you?

Rank the intermediaries from 0–5 using the above questions.

3. **How well do you understand their business, USPs and client characteristics?**
Mark from 0–5 to what extent you understand your intermediary's business, what they do for clients, which services they provide and how they support clients. What are the USPs of their firm? How does their firm fit within the competitive marketplace? Imagine that you witness a pitch they make to a new client. What would they highlight? How do they operate? What is unique on their side?

4. **Have you discussed how to pass on referrals to each other?**
Mark from 0–5 how well you have delivered on this point.

It is important that there is a good mutual under-standing of how referrals are given reciprocally and how to manage the relationship so that it works for you both. One of the reasons that intermediaries do not give referrals is their worry that if something went wrong, it could affect their client relationship. This is something you could discuss openly with the intermediary: how will you look after their client, without them feeling left out of the loop? This will be different for all your intermediaries, but it is important. For example, if they give you a referral, will they want to be copied in for a period of time or just kept abreast of the progress of the relationship? And crucially, if something goes a little wrong – for example, a client recommended by an intermediary gets frustrated at some point – do they want to be kept abreast of that? The more you clarify this area, the more comfortable your referrer will feel and the happier they will be to introduce you.

5. **Thinking laterally about who you could intro-duce to them and their firm, how you could help them?**

    Mark from 0–5 how well you have helped them in the past, finding clients for them and their firm. Have you thought of this intermediary as your best client, put yourself in their shoes and thought creatively and laterally, before going into a meeting with them, about possible clients to find for them? Is there anyone in your firm whom you can leverage to help find more clients or ask to come up with some ideas for you? Can you spread the word about this intermediary and what it does? How does it market itself to find more business? Have you asked for its pitch book so you can think laterally for them and their firm? Have you brainstormed directly with your intermediary about how you can think laterally for them, showing them your interest and efforts?

Think also about how you can help them personally. Does your firm or your contacts have any resources that could be helpful to them in their personal life?

As we know, if you rank highly on answering this question, it all goes towards cementing the relationship. The intermediary will then be happier to help you and to partner on finding quality referrals for you.

6. **Have you had a focused meeting on how this relationship can work for you both?**

Mark from 0–5 to what extent you have organized a specific meeting with your intermediary to cover:

- How well they understand your business, USPs and client characteristics?
- How well you understand their business, USPs and client characteristics?
- How much you have discussed how to pass on referrals to each other?
- How much lateral thinking you have done about who you could introduce to them and their firm?

Later in this chapter I have outlined how to initiate and choreograph a meeting with an intermediary to improve the relationship and increase the chances of a high-quality referral.

WORKSHEET

Assessing intermediaries

Rate each intermediary between 0 (minimum) and 5 (maximum)

Intermediary name								
How good are they at delivering referrals?								
How well does the intermediary understand your business, USPs and client characteristics?								
How well do you understand their business, USPs and client characteristics?								
Have you discussed how to pass on referrals to each other?								
Thinking laterally about who you could introduce to them and their firm, how you could help them?								

Intermediary name									
Have you had a focused meeting on how this relationship can work for you both?									

Download this worksheet and more resources at www.graham-eisner.com

Important decisions to be made after filling out the matrix

Ask yourself the following questions:

- How many of these intermediary relationships are truly delivering referrals?
- Which ones do you think have potential to give referrals and are truly worth the time and energy?
- And which ones is it sensible to give up and stop wasting time on?
- What have you learnt about yourself that you did not know before?
- How should you start to rethink your strategy around intermediaries?
- Can you brainstorm with your buddy or team mates on how to present yourself and your firm going forward to high-potential intermediaries, and how to learn what you need to from the intermediaries?
- How many intermediaries do you now want to be focusing on?
- What do you think is the right number for you, and why?

WORKSHEET

Following the assessment of intermediaries

IMs with most potential	Why do you believe in this potential?

Nurturing the intermediaries for the future

Now that you have been through the matrix, focus on the intermediaries remaining on the list that you want to nurture.

Exercise

Let's imagine that you have an intermediary in front of you and you can ask really direct questions. What would you most like to ask? (These are hypothetical questions and not ones you would actually ask in this way.) Below are some examples:

- Why are you not giving us referrals?
- Do you give any referrals to one or two of our competitors?
- If so, why are they higher on the list than we are?
- Do you really value us enough to refer one of your clients to us?
- What worries you about our firm that stops you giving us a referral?
- What would you say our values and USPs are?
- Do you know who our target client is?
- Do you know what differentiates us from our competitors?
- Can we have a list of all your clients?
- How do you introduce your firm to your clients, your differentiation in the marketplace, your values and USPs?
- What is in it for you to refer someone to us?
- What type of client would you like from us?
- What is your ideal client?

The point of doing this exercise is to understand what you really need and want to find out. You can actually ask all of these questions. There is just a way of phrasing that is more diplomatic but will get you the same results.

For example:

- There are a few things I would love to ask about our current relationship.
- I have noticed that we don't receive referrals from you. Would you mind giving me your sense of why this is the case, please?
- Would it be fair to say that one or two of our competitors are higher up the list to receive referrals from you than we are?
- I appreciate that in order for you to refer us, it is really important you have full information on our USPs and values. Do you feel that we give you this information? Is this what's holding us back?
- It would be useful to understand how you see referring to us as a benefit to you and your firm.
- In order to make this relationship work for us both, it would be great to speak about some specific clients that you have.

If you are just starting to build your business with intermediaries

If you don't have any clients and are looking for an intermediary who will refer you as a way to start building your business, a powerful way to do this is to show an intermediary a list of prospects that you will be approaching. This way, they will understand the types of clients you are trying to approach. A perfect moment to do this is when you are talking about yourself and your business and how you work.

Finding other excellent no-brainer intermediaries to work with

You have seen from the discussion above that some intermediary relationships are not a good use of your time and will not lead to a good referral. You probably need to cut them. However, if you are looking for a good intermediary with whom to start a relationship, begin by looking at the existing list of intermediaries servicing your clients. For example, using wealth management to illustrate, you will likely have some clients where you are in contact with their accountant or lawyer or trustee as part of your duties. In fact, you might have come into contact with many of these.

Think for a second. These intermediaries know you, maybe very well. They know how you work, the credibility of the firm you work for and its DNA and processes. One or more of them is quite possibly a perfect candidate with whom to grow your mutual relationship, in the quest for another client that they could introduce to you. As always, some work may be required to establish this potential. Find out whether this intermediary is already covered by one of your colleagues. You do not want to step on anyone's toes. Then, look at the intermediary business model and client base and amass data from their website and what you already know of them. Is it your instinct that they would be a good referrer?

If so, that is fantastic. You already have the relationship, so you need to approach them and say: 'Rosalind, it has been a pleasure working with you via our mutual client Katherine over the last six months/two years/10 years. I have an interesting idea I would like to run by you; one that might help us both in our businesses. When would suit you for a half-an-hour coffee?'

They will definitely say yes to this and you then proceed to approach this meeting in exactly the same way as you would with existing intermediaries. The areas to be covered are discussed below in 'Guide to the meeting'.

In the following worksheet, write a list of your clients on the left and then next to each client name, write the name of the lawyer who is your contact for the client account. Do the same for the accountant and trustee. Outside of the private client world, do the same thing for your industry. Write the clients on the left-hand side and fill in the current intermediaries that are servicing this client.

Now, with this list, look through and highlight the top 10 names where you have a good relationship. As explained above, these relationships could be expanded to find more clients.

WORKSHEET

Finding new intermediaries

Client name	Client's lawyers	Client's accountants	Client's trustees

How to improve intermediary relationships so they start to deliver

My suggestion is to organize a meeting to formalize the structure further. This meeting should last half an hour to one hour. The aim is to say something like: 'Samuel, we have a unique relationship and the aim of this meeting is to improve it for us both. I would love to look at learning more about your business and clients and the perfect prospects that you seek. Doing so will help me think more laterally and entrepreneurially about your business and who I can refer to you. I would also like to cover, if I have a referral for you, the best way to ensure that you have a meeting with them. I would also like to see if there is anything I could do to help you by giving you a greater insight into my business so that you understand what would make a perfect referral for it and how best to make that introduction.'

This is the kind of wording I would use at the beginning of the meeting, so it is clear what you are trying to achieve. It is really important to be methodical in this meeting. Think about the time you have. Let's assume it is one hour. It is important to be precise and really learn from what is said and take the relationship to the next level.

Guide to the meeting: setting the intermediary relationship on a new plane

2 mins: Introduction as set out just above.

10 mins: Ask questions and learn from the intermediary:

- Describe their firm: how many divisions, what industries do they focus on, where is the expertise?

- What differentiates their firm from competitors?
- What are their firms' values and USPs?
- Describe their perfect clients in terms of size, industry, geography, complexity.

10 mins: Describe your firm, how you service clients and what you do differently:

- Give clarity over your values and USPs.
- Define your perfect client and their complexity, geography and size.
- Outline how your firm differentiates itself from competitors.

5 mins: Introduce how you can find clients for the intermediary:

- Describe your own client base and the client base of your colleagues internally.
- Explore any other internal divisions it would be useful for them to be introduced to.
- Explore any other outside firms that you know would be useful for them to be put in touch with.
- Ask what other ideas they have as to how you could help them.

2 mins: Explore whether there are any resources of the firm that would be helpful for them personally.

5 mins: Cover how to manage the referral on both sides, if one is received.

5 mins: Introduce how they can find referrals for you:

- Ask which clients they are working with who could fit the criteria you outlined earlier.
- Only ask for one high-quality name to start with so that you can illustrate how you operate the relationship.

5 mins: Conclusion – how to really make this relationship work for you both over the short and long term.

Once you have found out this information, go for it in the meeting and ask for the referral.

This approach should have created a stronger bond and better understanding and willingness to collaborate. Now is the time to confront the topic of asking for a referral. I suggest you say something like: 'If we were going to start with one name to initiate this, and also so I can show you more closely how we work, who do you think that could be?' Notice that, as in the referral stages for clients, I recommend strongly that you ask only for one name.

If the intermediary does not have someone to work with you at that moment, it is important not to give up. Instead, take a long-term approach and ask: 'How can we work this together over the coming months so that we can find an opportunity to collaborate?'

This is the way to get the best out of your intermediary relationships. Next, we are going to look at how you can properly fulfil the potential of personal connections in your friends and family.

Chapter 10:

Summary Points

Asking for referrals from intermediaries

Challenge your existing intermediary strategy and make changes.

- **Does the intermediary you are focused on to deliver a referral actually deliver referrals?**
- **Do they truly understand what you and your business do for clients?**
- **Do you really understand their business and client base to know how to help them?**
- **Are you helping them enough to find clients?**
- **Have you both discussed how best to receive a referral from each other?**
- **Be brave and very direct with your questions to your intermediaries to find out what you need to improve the relationship.**
- **Be honest and follow the matrix to see which intermediaries to focus on and which to drop.**
- **If you are at an early stage of your career without clients or with very few, be brave and show intermediaries a list of clients you want to approach to see if they can help.**
- **Organize a structured meeting with an intermediary to address all points of the matrix and move the relationship to a new level regarding referrals.**

- **Look at the existing list of intermediaries servicing your clients that you already have contact with. This is a super-powerful group for new referrals. In the wealth management, private client world this would be lawyers/ accountants/trustees of existing clients.**

Asking Friends and Family

The American automobile executive Lee Iacocca memorably said: 'The only rock I know that stays steady, the only institution I know that works, is the family.'[13]

Friends and family members are an interesting group that we don't often approach for referrals. In this chapter, we will examine and discuss common reasons put forward that sometimes do not withstand closer scrutiny.

Below are some of the mindsets that hold us back from asking:

- Asking may compromise my relationship with them.
- It will be an uncomfortable conversation.
- They don't take me seriously in my profession; they only know me from our nights out, and we never talk about work.
- They have known me since my childhood.
- We only meet on social occasions. There would never be a time to ask.

The reality is that all our mindsets regarding family and friends are in our heads, painting enough of a negative picture to prevent us from asking for a referral. Let's address some of these mindsets individually.

---

[13] Available at: https://www.allgreatquotes.com/quote-250338/

1. **Asking may compromise my relationship with them**

   Is this really true? If you are honest with yourself, how much of that mindset arises from a feeling that this is taking you a little out of your comfort zone and that you have never had this kind of conversation before? Will it affect the relationship or just take it into a certain other direction?

2. **It will be an uncomfortable conversation**

   Does it need to be uncomfortable? How much of this is your mind telling you how it thinks it will be for you and for them? We will ensure this is not the case by following the ideas and suggestions below.

3. **They don't take me seriously in my profession; they only know me from our nights out, and we never talk about work**

   This may be true but it is only a perception of your mind. If indeed this is the case, they will tell you so when you speak. What will you have lost? By following the steps below, you can quickly move away from this perception.

4. **They have known me since my childhood**

   This may be true, but again, this obstacle exists more in your head than anywhere else. Are you 100% sure this disqualifies you in their eyes? You think your family and friends will only look at you from one perspective and that this cannot change, so in a way you are always going to be stuck in the past with them. But if we follow the advice below, we move away from this scenario.

The key to overcome all the above mindsets

Take the person and the relationship out of the normal positions that they occupy – for example, family gatherings in the pub or at sporting events. Contact can easily be made with a family or friend through an email saying that you would love to have a business chat with them and asking if they have time for a coffee next week.

It is important to pick a time and location that reflect the sort of conversation you would like to have. It makes sense to have this meeting on a weekday during working hours at a location near their work that is quiet and has a casual atmosphere.

The coffee and how to choreograph it

First, there will be some social chat. Then move on to what you want to say by telling the friend or family member that you're aware that you are meeting in a different context from your usual relationship, but you would like to explore how you could help each other in a business format.

Ask if you can find out more about what they do at their company. As they tell you about that, think for 10 minutes or so about how you can help this person via an introduction or some kind of support. Is there one person you know who could help them?

After having a mini-conversation about how you can help, you can draw that conversation to an end by telling the person that you are really interested in what they do and are going to try and think of ways that you can help them and their business. The aim here is to forge a business connection by being genuinely interested in what they do and finding a way of helping them, even if it is not immediately.

Forge a business connection

This is also an opportunity to take this family member or friend into the groove of seeing what you are like in a business format: how you sit, how you listen, what you ask, what you understand from what they say and your business intuition. Ask insightful questions about their business and offer wise thoughts about how you could possibly help them.

In 10 minutes, which is the maximum that this should take, you can achieve a lot of the above and move your more formal developing relationship to another place. This then sets you up to progress by sharing a few details about your own line of work and your firm.

You have an opportunity to give a really concise and clear description of the firm you are working for and what you are doing within the company's business. You can also give a brief insight into how you got there. It is effectively a subtle sell about you. Quickly, efficiently and impressively, this is your opportunity to highlight the strengths of your firm, which in turn immediately gives you added credibility.

At this point, they are likely to see you differently and have a deeper understanding of how seriously you take your career, how much it means to you and what matters to you in your line of work.

Asking for the referral and how to follow up

After you have gained this person's trust and understanding, it will not be hard to disclose that you are in the process of building your business slowly, but with the right sort of clients, and wondering if they know of one contact that they would be happy to refer you to.

Hopefully, since you have followed my recommended process, this should not feel uncomfortable. After the meeting, you should follow the normal follow-up guidelines, as given in Chapter 9.

With a family member or friend, it could feel more natural to just let things lie and not push this request any further but, as we have said in Chapter 8 on preparing your client, now is the crux – the important part. They want to help you and you need to ensure that it will actually happen. You therefore go through the follow-up process mentioned in Chapter 9.

They will have thought of someone or asked for time to think about it, and we know the two responses. Your reply will not be so formal this time. If they cannot think of someone, thank them for thinking about it, tell them you really appreciate the effort and ask if you can send them a quick email over the next week to see if one name *has* come up.

Notice that I am assuming that they will have actually thought of someone in the interim. From my experience, this is much more effective than saying you will check to see if they have had a chance to think of someone.

It is subtly pushier, but the likelihood is that they will indeed have made the effort to think of someone for you. However, you need to stay in control of the opportunity. If they say that they have indeed thought of somebody and may ask that person the next time they see them, you do risk losing control. To avoid this, I suggest that you need to be brave in the moment and ask if you can contact the friend or family member the following week.

The obvious and easy thing to do is to hear that there is a name, let them make the introduction as they see fit and wait for the consequence. However, to take control and ensure that an introduction is offered in a way that gives you the greatest chance of success, it is best to give the friend or family member some guidance on how you would like them to proceed.

First, if they have thought of someone, you can ask a couple of questions about their identity and background.

Second, a reminder from Chapter 8:

- 'What has worked very well for me in the past is …'
- 'What would be very powerful for me is …'
- 'What I have seen from past experience and would be most helpful for me right now is …'

Ask if they would be able to call the person they have thought of and tell them why they believe it would make sense to have a short meeting with you: 'I have known Graham for X years. He is working for X firm. I have great respect and trust for Graham in his business role and the firm he is working with. I recommend you meet him for a brief coffee or video call to hear more about what he is doing. I think you will find it very useful and insightful.'

Then ask if you can send a three-way email linking you all up. Once they have done this, you can tell them that you will take it from there.

The last thing to ask, in order to respect your relationship, is how much they would like to be kept in the loop, obviously taking confidentiality into account.

Finally, if necessary, you can ask if you could possibly give them a little nudge if you have not heard anything in a week or so.

I have found a further benefit to asking for referrals from friends and family; it is a gentle way to test whether that person might actually be interested in your services. You can describe your ideal client and, sometimes, they find it applies to them. This is effective without being pushy.

Exercise

List your top five family members and friends to ask for a referral:

1.

2.

3.

4.

5.

Chapter 11:

Summary Points

Asking friends and family

- Family and friends are a strong source of referrals.
- There will be mindsets that hold you back, but none must do so.
  Don't take seriously thoughts such as:
  - ○ 'They have known me since childhood.'
  - ○ 'They don't take me seriously in the workplace.'
- Make sure that you organize the meeting one-on-one in a business environment.
- Find ways to give back to this friend or family member so that you can reciprocate the help they are giving to you.

Think as laterally as you can with friends and family – who might they be able to introduce you to?

Make a list of family and friends and put next to each name two people you would like to be introduced to, either a direct client prospect or a key intermediary.

Chapter 12

Making the Most of
Internal Referrals

The civil rights leader Martin Luther King Jr said memorably: 'Every man lives in two realms: the internal and the
external.'[14]

In the early 1990s, Goldman Sachs operated quite a flat
structure. One day, a new chairman for Europe was installed,
and I quickly knocked on his door to set up a 10-minute
meeting. Clearly, he wanted Goldman Sachs to acquire all
new forms of business. But he would not introduce a friend
unless he felt fully comfortable with the person and team
he was introducing this person to. Therefore, to achieve a
client referral, I had work to do to gain that trust. He became
in my mind my best client. I treated him with great professionalism, introducing the resources of our division to him,
as if he did not know anything about it. In truth, although he
was chairman, he did not know the minutiae of how this area
within the firm operated.

A strategy for internal referrals

Is there anyone outside of your particular working division
in the firm who is working at a senior level and might know
of a potential prospect for you? Perhaps it is their friend,

---

[14] Available at: www.brainyquote.com/quotes/martin_luther_king_
jr_691619

neighbour, someone on the board of a charity they are connected to or somebody at their sports club or cultural association? Of course, it might be someone they have come into contact with via the business line they are involved in, such as the firm's head of compliance, logistics or events.

I normally suggest that it is best to start by thinking about only the very senior people, so let's start with the partners of the firm. The partners own equity, so they have a vested interest in increasing the firm's profitability. Of course, the rung below the partners is also important. Those on it could become partners, and if they have been there a long time, they will also have a natural interest in helping you grow your business. Equally, if the firm is not equity-based, the senior management or the senior leaders of different business lines are all interested in growing the firm's broad client base.

The common denominator here – especially if it is a friend whom this work colleague is introducing – is their natural reluctance for it to affect their relationship if something were to go wrong. Also, if they have a contact in a business they are involved in, the same scenario exists. Is it worth the risk to introduce them to you? If something were to go wrong, it might affect the business they bring into other parts of the firm.

The answer with internal referrals is to treat them like clients or prospects: give them confidence about what you and your division deliver for potential clients. This way we typically can improve the relationship and identify opportunities without compromising the friendliness of the relationship. Remember, they too have a job, goals, hurdles and might be grateful for your help – and they too might be happy to create mutually beneficial relationships around them. Even if no such relationships are possible, your asking shows that you are willing to support them.

Stages for asking for referrals from internal introducers

1. **Discover your top five internal introducers**

   Make a list. Who are the natural introducers, the ones who definitely will have some potential clients? For me at Goldman Sachs, the chairman was clearly a very influential man who would know similarly powerful and very wealthy individuals. It was also clear that I had to get to know the people who worked in different divisions; for example, where Goldman Sachs was building relationships with private companies to raise capital at some future date.

   Colleagues in these areas would be spending a lot of time with entrepreneurs and with other directors, illustrating Goldman Sachs' strengths and qualities. It therefore made great sense for the entrepreneurs to be introduced at the right moment to the private client area to be advised on future wealth. However, I needed to make sure that this introduction was seamless, avoiding any fear or other emotions that could hold colleagues back from making introductions.

   The above are two obvious types of person to ask, but outside of them, make a list to help you think laterally about internal prospects. Write down the names of the senior people internally:

   - someone who, by virtue of what they do, would know a potential client;
   - someone running a business line with clients who could be interesting to you;
   - someone who is a networker and is definitely meeting potential prospects;

- someone in a very senior position who went to the same school/university as you;
- someone simply in a very senior position;
- someone who loves the sport you love and/or plays it;
- someone from the same town or country;
- someone with similar hobbies or interests.

Once you have ascertained the top five, you can move on to:

2. **Making contact**

This is relatively easy to do. You could either walk straight up to them, or if they are very senior and less approachable, you might speak to their secretary – this is easily done by saying you have something to ask a given executive and could you go into their diary for a five-minute appointment?

If they are approachable, I do not suggest sending an email. It is simply a case of finding them in their office, or in the building, and telling them that you would love to run a few things by them and asking if you can be put in their diary for a brief coffee or video call for 15 minutes when it suits them. This should definitely lead to the two of you committing to a time to get together.

3. **Plan and choreograph the meeting**

This meeting is important, just like external client ones. Plan and choreograph it and set a goal. Before you go into the meeting, think about what the person does in the firm. Think laterally about how you could help them in their division. Think of them as your best client or someone who might become such. Brainstorm how you could help them.

Depending on how well you know this person, you might start on their background and what led them to the firm. Once this is done, after about two minutes, you can start introducing your area of the firm.

4. **What to say**

   Tell your colleague that you are not sure how familiar they are with your division, and how it manages and looks after client relationships. Then tell them briefly what your division is trying to achieve. Give them some details they would not know about, reference the trust and service that you give clients and then focus on how you manage the relationship. Mention also how well you are doing in the marketplace and that the firm's approach in this area is unique and very well-received by clients. Give some sense of how the USPs and values of the firm run through the veins of your area or division.

   In those five minutes, you are highlighting succinctly the real benefits of how your division looks after clients, what you achieve for them, and how well the clients feel looked after. You are giving your colleague some insights, plus a very comfortable backdrop to the next part of the conversation.

   The next stage is saying that you would like to explore how you can help the person you are meeting. Think about this before going in. Think entrepreneurially and laterally. For the person I targeted in Goldman Sachs' Principal Investment Area, I devoted time and the resource of my assistant to help him build his business. I also facilitated his making a presentation to our group so he could generate more leads of potential businesses to invest in. I also became his conduit to the private client group in which I worked when he needed to disseminate information.

It does not matter if they thank you but say they have no need of your assistance. They will respect the fact that you suggested it and that will help them to feel positive about helping you.

5. Set up the scene to ask for a referral
Next, you need to set up asking for a referral, saying that your area of the firm has some spare capacity and you would love to ask for his or her help on just one thing. Then give a very clear example of what your perfect client looks like.

At this point you need to ascertain what relationship you have developed in this short space of time. How senior is the person you are speaking to? Would it be best to end this short meeting there and then and suggest a follow-up meeting, including a five-minute visit from your head of wealth management? This is exactly what I did in the second meeting with the new Goldman Sachs' chairman, and it paid dividends.

Tell your colleague that, although you have only just met them properly, you would love to explore if there is someone you can think of together over the coming month, who they would be happy to introduce to your part of the business. Reinforce that you fully understand the importance of them being 100% comfortable that you will look after their existing relationship, especially if it is with a highly private family or another sensitive client. Then ask if they would like to be kept in the loop, of course respecting confidentiality.

6. Sense the response

Listen carefully to the reaction of your internal colleague as you are telling them all of this. Do you sense a slight pullback? At this point I would definitely be adding a disclaimer that you recognize why some people within the firm may be reluctant to give a referral. If it is a friend or neighbour and something goes wrong, would it affect their relationships? If it is a client on their side of the firm and something goes wrong, would it affect the business they are already doing?

The point here is that, as you get to know a potential internal referrer, just as with a potential client, the whole process has to be very well understood from all sides, with the relationship only entered into if both parties are happy. Clearly, in handling this relationship there needs to be some highly professional hand-holding.

Tell the colleague you are glad to have met them and had this discussion and would love to have another small coffee meeting in a week or two to discuss it further. Suggest that another meeting will give them the opportunity to ask any questions they might have as to how your division operates, in order to make them fully comfortable.

Alternatively, if there is no sense of pullback, suggest that if they could make a short call to the prospect to introduce you and your area of the firm, and then send a three-way email to all of you to make the introduction, that would be a very powerful outcome for you.

Asking for referrals from former colleagues who now work at another firm

Do you have any former work colleagues who you got on very well with, and who appreciated how you handle clients, valued your work ethics and basically trusted you? These people might have shifted career and moved into a senior role in an intermediary firm.

The point is: people move on and their networking changes, and the circles they move in change. But your relationship remains strong and you can definitely benefit from this for an introduction. It doesn't matter if you haven't had any contact for five or 10 years. People do not forget. Therefore, contact them via email, LinkedIn, WhatsApp or some other messaging platform and tell them that you know it has been a while, but you would love to meet up over coffee or have an online meeting to see if there is a way you could help each other. Say that you have been thinking laterally about this and it would be great to take it further. Ask when it might suit them to meet.

Brainstorm how you can help them

Find out what this former colleague does now, brainstorm with a colleague or by yourself, and come up with a way you could help them. Even if what you say isn't what they need right now, it shows that you have thought about them. You have also given them a reason to meet you, apart from just a catch-up. This way, you need not feel even slightly embarrassed or pushy if you bring up asking for a referral in the meeting.

How you then handle this meeting is similar to how you should approach family and friends in Chapter 11. The point here is that we are always looking for the warm opportunity; the one that we perhaps did not take advantage of before.

Exercise

List your top five internal colleagues you could ask for a referral:

1.

2.

3.

4.

5.

List your top five former work colleagues you could ask for a referral:

1.

2.

3.

4.

5.

Ask for a referral even after being rejected by the referred prospect at the first meeting

So, you carried out the process I have described, successfully prepared for asking a client/intermediary/friend or family member or internal colleague for a referral, followed up well, achieved the referral and then approached the referred person and successfully arranged a meeting.

You carried out a good meeting, but the person tells you it is not for them and gives you a reason why. It may not even be the right reason, as of course it is their prerogative to throw you a swerve ball. But this does not matter, because you tried.

You also now have an opportunity. You were introduced by someone whom this person trusts and respects. You then built that trust further by having a great meeting, showing the values of your firm, quality, professionalism, passion and belief in your firm and its products and services. All this will only have shown the referred person what a good person you are to work with and how great your firm is.

They may not choose to pursue a client relationship at this time, but this still gives you a perfect moment to say that it has been a pleasure meeting them and that you have had a very productive meeting. You completely respect and appreciate that it may not be the right time for them to work with your firm. But you also wonder if there is one person/ company they know who might benefit from the products, service and strong relationships that your firm offers.

Basically, what do you have to lose? This is a completely appropriate question and you can only gain by asking it. The referred person may feel a touch guilty that they do not want to work with you, so may be only too pleased to help in this other way.

Remember, connecting people does not come naturally to everyone. Yet nearly everyone enjoys connecting people when it is mutually beneficial. By checking with people whether or not there is a possibility to make a connection, and being willing to accept 'no' as an answer, you might be doing them a favour.

Cross-selling internal referrals

These are very important and powerful referrals for your business. Cross-selling internal referrals use strong existing client relationships to introduce your business's services or products to other divisions within the client's company.

Why does cross-selling not happen?

Sometimes, this is related to a lack of team spirit in your business to naturally help other product divisions. Alternatively, leadership in the business can simply lack the DNA that pushes client-facing executives to constantly think laterally when in front of clients, always considering whether there is another of the firm's services that might be useful to them. It can also be financially related, with client-facing people feeling no motivation to cross-sell. It can also be related to a lack of understanding of the other products and services that your business offers.

The reality is that cross-selling referrals probably represent one of the easiest ways for your firm to grow its revenue and profits. The firm has a relationship with a client, and they have illustrated well in one business line how they operate, differentiate themselves from the competition, their professionalism, service, etc. There will be members of the team serving this client who are well-liked and trusted, and it would be fairly easy for them to broach the subject of being introduced to another part of the client firm.

I have helped businesses including design agencies, financial consultancy firms, security risk consultancy firms, accountants and legal firms succeed with this technique.

Stages

It is important to be thoughtful about your client's business and think strategically about the needs of another division of that business. Then:

- **Try to identify the senior decision-maker that you would like your client to introduce you to.**
- **Introduce a bridge line.** This is similar to the bridge line for the client relationship in Chapter 6. You could ask your client for holistic feedback on the relationship, knowing it would be positive, or you could refer to the values and USPs of your firm that you know the client has experienced. Alternatively, if there is an important piece of work you have done for your client recently, you can refer to this. Or finally, you could refer to the fact that there has been some restructuring internally and there is now some spare capacity in the business. All of the above are powerful bridge lines and lead very seamlessly, as shown in Chapter 6, to asking for the help of their client on one thing.
- **Bring your client's attention to another division of your firm.** You would give a few lines and background to illustrate how capable and strong this division is in the marketplace and how it would benefit their contact Mr/Mrs X, running the relevant division, to have a brief meeting to hear about the products/

services. You would love to ask to be introduced. It is very rare for a client to decline this, and they would be very happy to help you. It is true sometimes that either your mind will tell you – or perhaps your client may bring up a concern – that the focus on the current work you are doing with this client will be compromised. You can allay this fear very easily by talking about the team splits and how there is an abundance of capacity due to restructuring. Mostly this obstacle takes place in your head, and the client will be very willing to help. Remember from Chapter 5 that presentation, posture and body language are equally important to put across your request with absolute confidence and resoluteness.

- **Listen well** to the client's response that will normally express a willingness to help.
- **Help your client in the way they will approach their colleague heading the other division.** We learnt the importance of this in Chapters 8 and 9. Will they phone this person directly, will they see them in person? They will need to mention the strength of the relationship and introduce you well, to ensure an introduction.
- **Confirm that they carried out the referral** and then follow up with the colleague of the client once it has been set up. You can also ask, if you have not heard anything in a week or so, would they mind you giving them a nudge to remind them as you know how busy they can get.

Chapter 12:

Summary Points

Making the most of internal referrals

- Your internal colleagues want to help you. You only need to ask.
- Help them in some way. Make it a reciprocal relationship.
- Expressing your thanks and gratitude for the help of this internal colleague is very important to ensure that they will help again.
- Treat internal colleagues like your best client and build the trust in the same way as with a client.
- If you succeed in getting a meeting with a referred prospect from a client, intermediary or an internal colleague and it becomes clear in your meeting that they will not become a client, ask that prospect for a referral anyway.
- Take advantage of cross-selling internal referrals. These internal referrals use strong existing client relationships to introduce your business' services or products to other divisions within the client's company.

Chapter 13

Using Networking to Ask for Referrals

Apple magnate Steve Jobs was convinced that 'about half of what separates successful entrepreneurs from the non-successful ones is pure perseverance'.[15] Networking is not as rich a hunting ground for potential referrals as the external or internal opportunities I described earlier. However, it can still be very useful. We all spend a lot of time networking and you could be someone who is constantly looking for opportunities, whether on a plane or at a drinks party, club or association meeting or an organized event for clients where they bring along a friend. For others, networking comes less naturally but they still look to attend events, meet people and try to use these environments to find ways to grow their business. However, the majority of people go to a number of events but don't plan very well, are not interested in making a great effort or are not sure what to do and don't really follow up the connections made. The methodology outlined below will increase the likelihood that networking events will get you referrals.

---

[15] Available at: www.google.co.uk/amp/s/www.businessinsider. com/instant-mba-passion-and-perseverance-are-what-separates-successful-entrepreneurs-from-failures%3famp

Prepare before the event

Try to focus on who is going to be there and whom you might meet. You may already know who will be coming. Otherwise, it is a good idea to get hold of the list of participants before attending. Try and meet the event organizer beforehand to talk through who will be there. Of course, this person could also introduce you to people you want to meet at the event. This will automatically break the ice and add credibility.

Focus on 10 people you really want to meet

When you arrive, you need to work out where these people are. The next step is to somehow approach them individually. This can seem a brave thing to do and it does take effort and involves working the room. But if you want to spend some time networking, it is best to do so efficiently and make your efforts worthwhile. Once you have located a person you want to talk to at an event, introduce yourself with one or two lines about the event, asking how they are enjoying it and what they are aiming to get out of it. Talk about their business and what they do, and ask insightful questions. They will ask what you do, so that is your opportunity. If they do not, then you will need to bring it up yourself. After about five minutes, you can say: 'It has been a pleasure meeting you. It would be great to learn more about your business and share more about what we are doing at X firm. Now is probably not the perfect time. Let's put a time in to meet for a coffee in the next couple of weeks.'

This is the crucial line; it is a way of not being sucked into effectively having a first meeting at the event, where there is distraction, and it is also a positively polite yet affirmative way to try and put a meeting in the diary.

I would suggest this is said quite casually and in a relaxed tone, not sounding pre-planned or making them feel under any pressure. It also needs to make sense why you are suggesting this, and this is clear if you have carried out the first part of your interaction well. You gained trust, were likeable and insightful at the event and, through your research on this person, you asked interesting and intelligent questions about their business. All of this can be achieved in five minutes, when cleverly planned. It is similar to the impressions you are making in a first meeting with a prospect.

Once they've agreed to meet again, try to arrange there and then at the event when to meet, or get their business card and tell them you'll email the next day to suggest a couple of times to meet. Sometimes when you write the next day, they may not reply. My suggestion here is to follow up with a phone call after a day or two. It's really important to strike while the iron is hot. If a potential prospect showed enthusiasm at the event to meet you again, this will decline quickly over time, as the function's momentum diminishes. Enthusiasm has a half-life, with the chance of success-fully being able to meet such a person for a coffee roughly halving for each week that goes by. I still advise persisting. They did say it would be good to have a meeting, so you only need to remind them of that when you do eventually make contact.

Remember, if you phone and the contact does not answer, do not leave a message. Try again two days later.

Using LinkedIn to obtain referrals

Clearly LinkedIn can be used intelligently to find very warm leads. These could be any of the following:

- Reminders of friends/former work colleagues with whom you have had little or no contact for some years but who have moved into influential positions within a company or an intermediary; have become entrepreneurial and super-wealthy; or are networkers and influencers.
- Go through the names of your current contacts; think about the industry they are working in and whether they could be an interesting intermediary for you. Think about what their passions are, and whether this might have brought them into contact with some great client prospects. Are they possibly on the board of some key influential charities or company? For the wealth manager, is your contact into art or some other prospect-rich cultural area? Is your contact influential or a patron in a key institution?
- Look at the profiles of existing clients to see who they know. Are there any other potential clients whom they might know?

Fear and embarrassment

There will also be other ways in which LinkedIn could help you find some great referrals. With all these, you may think it is a bit creepy, pushy or intruding to get in contact with this client/friend or X work colleague and say you saw the name of someone that they knew on LinkedIn. However, this is only in your mind and not something to be concerned with. You are being entrepreneurial and they will respect this.

What I suggest is be honest and see excellent leads for perfect referrals as exactly what they are. You just need to get these friends, former colleagues and clients to make the referral for you.

Dos and don'ts

What I would *not* suggest doing is writing a LinkedIn message (or InMail if you have paid for the more expensive LinkedIn subscriptions), asking contacts or clients if they could make an introduction. If it really could be an excellent referral, this is a waste of time, as they probably will not reply. I believe it is necessary to arrange a coffee or a brief video call.

Taking action and following up

Friends or former work colleagues

Use the same approach that I suggested in Chapter 11. Send an email, WhatsApp message or another form of communication, to say you would love to have a quick coffee or a video call to reconnect and also have a business chat. Mention that you have been thinking of a couple of ways in which the two of you can help each other.

The approach is similar to the approach in Chapter 11. Once you are having the coffee or video call, find out about what they are doing, and think laterally on the spot and before you meet, as to how you could possibly help them.

Depending on the history of your contact – and the length of time since you have last been in touch or spoken – you will need to bring them up to date with what you are doing now, and build up a great story around why you are working where you are. Tell them about your excellent firm and its resources and the business you are building. This should lead nicely into asking for a referral. Then, move on to the one person that you would love their help in introducing you to.

In the same way as you would for a client, manage the process of how they get in touch with the person they will refer you to, and how you will follow up. Remembering your lack of contact over the years, they may not have your request at the top of their to-do list. They want to help you but need help to ensure that it happens.

Clients

If you have seen a prospect who has great potential for a referral on a client's LinkedIn page, I suggest that you bring it up face-to-face, or on the next video call that you have. This would take the same format as always for a client: finding a bridge line and asking for help on one name only and following the 7 steps as outlined in Chapters 6, 7, 8 and 9.

Other possibilities to get in touch with a less-known LinkedIn contact

You may have made a number of new LinkedIn contacts by simply finding interesting links via your existing network. You asked to be connected and they accepted because they saw that you came via a close contact of theirs. At this point you are a little bit closer to them. However, this is not close enough to send an InMail and ask to meet.

Instead, you could write a message reminding them of how you connected and of your mutual contacts. This will make it warm and ensure that they take your message seriously and respond. Explain that you have a couple of mutually beneficial things you would like to bring up with them. You would love to arrange a two-minute call. Ask them to let you know when suits them, or say you will try and get in contact over the coming days.

This is relaxed and yet shows you are keen to get in touch and that you will. This will prompt them to respond and arrange a quick call. Before this call, think about the business they are in and try to think laterally about how you can help them with a useful introduction.

You will notice that I am not asking for permission to give this person a call. I am using the assumed credibility you have by coming into contact with this person via someone that he or she has known for some time. If you ask for permission for a call, they will probably not reply.

However, now that you have given yourself permission, you can call their business number and when they pick up, you are not a stranger and this is not a cold call. You can say at once who is calling and remind them that you have come into contact through your mutual connection. Tell them that you know that there are lots of interesting areas where you could mutually help each other and it would be great to talk about it over a quick coffee. Suggest meeting some time over the next week.

Again, quite a lot of positive assumptions are used here, but this should work to arrange the coffee. Then, when you are having this coffee meeting, you can approach it as I have advised in Chapter 10.

Prioritizing and categorizing your LinkedIn contact list

One final point I would make about using LinkedIn is about prioritizing and categorizing. We all have hundreds of contacts and of course we only have a certain amount of time.

First, I would print out your list of LinkedIn contacts, on big sheets of paper. Create categories such as:

1. Clients
2. Former clients
3. Current intermediaries

4. Family
5. Friends
6. Former work colleagues
7. Contacts you initiated via a mutual contact
8. Incoming contact requests.

Number these categories as above. Then next to each contact name put the relevant category number. Then make individual lists with the category headings and all the relevant names underneath. Next, prioritize within these individual category lists. Now we are ready to be commercial and practical to use our LinkedIn contact list very effectively with good time management.

Also, we cannot have a coffee with all these people. For some, it will make more sense to have a video call. I would still use the same process I have explained above, but it can all be achieved in 15 minutes, and of course this is saving a great deal of time. There will also be some LinkedIn connections that you could contact via a voice phone call and not on video. This is about managing your list and deciding.

Chapter 13:

Summary Points

Using networking to ask for referrals

Networking at an event

- **Prepare before the event, finding out who is going and who you want to meet.**
- **Be ruthless about your time management. Focus on efficient prospecting before, at and following networking events.**
- **At the events, approach your prospects, keep it very short. Just get the meeting and then move off the subject.**
- **Use the line: 'Now is not the time. Let's put in a time to meet for a coffee/video call in the next couple of weeks.'**
- **Follow up immediately, strike while the iron is hot. Enthusiasm has a half-life, their enthusiasm to meet you will diminish by a half, each week.**

Before the next event/conference/dinner you attend, ask yourself:

- *'How am I preparing differently for this event?'*
- *'How is my plan different? What am I doing that I have not done before?'*
- *'How am I approaching the follow-up to this event differently from before?'*

Using LinkedIn

- **Use LinkedIn to establish which of your contacts, personally known or not known by you, are NOW in an influential position where they might know one high-quality prospect.**
- **Use LinkedIn to establish which clients have a contact who could be a prospect.**
- **Do not write to these contacts asking them to make an introduction.**
- **Organize a coffee with your contact and then duplicate the advice given in previous chapters to achieve the referral.**
- **Prioritize your LinkedIn contacts, categorizing all your contacts into lists:**

1. Clients
2. Former clients
3. Current intermediaries
4. Family
5. Friends
6. Former work colleagues
7. Contacts you initiated via a mutual contact
8. Incoming contact requests.

Asking in a Pandemic

The first draft of this book was completed in February 2020 and, of course, since then we have had government-imposed lockdowns. We all know the world will be different afterwards. In this postscript, I want to highlight what will have changed regarding referrals and also what modifications might need to be made.

Asking for client referrals

Depending on when you pick up this book, the way of working due to COVID-19 will be different. If there is a universal vaccine and/or a form of testing and safety measures imposed in offices, client meetings and interactions will all occur, perhaps with some differences from before the pandemic. In terms of asking for referrals, however, nothing will really change. The client relationship that has been sought with you and the delivery of the relationship or client mandate remains the same.

Before a universal vaccine is available, it is clear there will be less interaction than before, fewer face-to-face client meetings and fewer gatherings, meetings with friends and family and intermediaries. It will be a time that is less connected.

However, your business will be running and you will still be seeking to grow it. The reality is that the growing of businesses is not stopping, and clients still need your services. They may even require them because they are unhappy with how a competitor of yours has acted during COVID-19. Or they might have had an event or a demand that has led them to desire your services.

Many of your competitors will be reluctant to reach out and ask for referrals. Therefore, by using these techniques, you are more likely to have an advantage over your competition.

It is important that you become confident with and adept at using video conferencing. Your image, online presence, posture, delivery and preparation are all paramount. Being able to connect effectively remotely is a skill. It is important to control the meeting in the same way as you would face-to-face. You still need an agenda, to operate excellent time-keeping and to ensure you have covered all you want to.

The biggest block to asking for a referral during a video conference with a client will be in your mind. This book has shown that everyone has mindset blocks that hold them back from asking for a referral. There will be some fear on your part, and your mind may suggest that now is not the time to be asking for a referral. Your mind will tell you that you might as well wait until you meet the contacts face-to-face, for fear of messing it up.

However, referrals should and can still be asked for. I would 100% recommend asking for them over a live video link. It is true that the criteria for people to ask in the context of a video link may change slightly. I would suggest focusing on clients you know well, have a good relationship with and who have appreciated the services, values and trust of your firm. Such clients will have met you a number of times before, so it should not make a great deal of difference if you ask them for a referral on a video conference call, following the methodology laid out in this book. Of course, one difference will be that a client may suggest when they make the introduction that you meet the referred person for the first time via a video link, rather than in person.

With clients who have not known you or your firm for very long, I would not ask for a referral at this stage, waiting until either face-to-face meetings resume or until you have created a stronger relationship. Hopefully in the periods of lockdown and uncertainty, you continued to hold the hand of your clients through the challenging times, illustrating your ability and that of your firm to support your client in the way they wanted. If carried out well, this may even have enhanced and deepened the relationship and further grown trust. Hopefully, the parameters set by the client were also being met during this tough time.

Therefore, I would not suggest changing any of the methodology outlined in this book. You need not even mention COVID-19, other than to state what it has shown you about values and trust. This can then move nicely into one of the suggested bridge lines before asking for a referral.

Asking intermediaries

Asking intermediaries for referrals should likewise not change in the current climate, though I would only ask for referrals from intermediaries you know at least reasonably well. Only ask on a video link and not over the phone or via email. I would not change anything else. The intermediary may have some questions as to how you and your company have dealt with COVID-19. If they do not, there is no need to bring it up. Ultimately, they are making a referral based on what they know of you and your firm, in the time you have been getting to know them.

Internal referrals

With internal referrals, I would still set up internal video conferencing when arranging the first interaction. You might be meeting them for the first or second time. If they are going to help you, you need to see them, and they need to see you. They will then believe your willingness to help the friend or business colleague that you want them to introduce you to, and see the authenticity of your wanting to find ways to help them.

Friends and family

Friends and family know and trust you and will therefore react on a video conference with the same enthusiasm to help you as they would have done previously.

Postscript:

Summary Points

Asking in a pandemic

- Asking for a referral does not change due to the pandemic. You can ask all the clients and intermediaries.
- The only main change is that it is less easy to ask when the relationship is in an early stage.
- Becoming confident using video conferencing and utilizing this tool well while asking for a referral is important.
  Practise this and ask for feedback from your colleagues after meetings.
- Highlight the illustration of your firm's values and USPs during COVID-19.

Contacting the Author

I would love to hear how you get on, putting these guidelines into action. To get in touch, contact me at graham@graham-eisner.com. You can also visit my site www.graham-eisner.com to watch the free-to-view short videos of my methodology and get updates on online workshops to join.

Summary Points

Overview from each chapter

Chapter 1: Why ask?

Referrals are a hidden gem. This book will give you the individual strategies to double your business.

Currently:

- **You find it difficult to ask.**
- **You forget to ask.**
- **You are unsure how to ask.**

This book will give you:

- **a strategy for each client/intermediary;**
- **the confidence to ask;**
- **methods to think laterally;**
- **a willingness and motivation to change.**

How to maximize your use of this book:

- **Use the worksheets to exercise your memory and new habits.**
- **Use the summary points to re-visit and engage with your new-found methodology.**

Chapter 2: The number one strategy

Why referrals should be the number one strategy to grow your business:

- **Referrals reduce your costs of acquisition of new business.**
- **Referrals reduce your anxiety about finding new business.**
- **Referrals help you focus on high-probability prospects, thereby reducing time wasted.**

Ask yourself:

How much anxiety and stress stems from the way you currently try to find new clients?

How many new prospects have you truly acquired from the methods you use?

How much time have you spent in doing so?

- **Referrals mean less pricing pressure from an incoming referred client.**
- **Referred prospects are easier and quicker to close.**
- **There is a networking effect. Clients who have been referred will themselves refer.**
- **Referrals increase the loyalty of existing clients who give a referral.**
- **Referrals increase the enjoyment in your job.**

Chapter 3: Why people don't ask

While people in sales only ask for referrals from 20% of their clients, 60% of their client base would actually be happy to offer them one.

Why we don't ask for referrals:

- **We don't agree with their importance.**
- **We have a subconscious fear of rejection.**
- **We forget to ask.**

Our mindset gets in the way of asking:

- **Fear on many levels leads to procrastination.**
- **We make assumptions about clients and their reactions.**
- **We are too confident that referrals will simply be given.**

All these mindsets are in our heads and none of them need hold us back from asking for a referral.

Create a prioritized client referral list.

Chapter 4: Make it easier for yourself

- Give clients better service and contact. Ensure hand-holding in difficult times. Follow up effectively and be aware of bringing the right resources of the firm to your client.
- Empower yourself. Turn negativity in your mind to positivity around referrals.
- Be aware of the positive language changes you use in meetings where you ask for referrals. Repeat them and note them down.
- Appreciate and be passionate about the values and USPs you offer clients.
- Organize your time better.
- Get a buddy system working around referral support.
- Who will you ask to buddy with you? Can you start this next week?
- Be bold and more ambitious. You may think you already have challenging targets. Increase them by 20% and ask yourself how you can achieve that. If you were convinced that referrals would help you achieve these targets, would that make it easier for you to ask for referrals?
- Discuss with your client how to keep them up to date about their referred friend/colleague/contact, always respecting confidentiality.

Chapter 5: Improving your confidence

- **Omit 'maybe' or 'possibly' when asking for a referral in a meeting.**
- **Assume a confident, upright seated posture.**
- **Don't let your eyes wander when asking for a referral.**
- **Use breathing and other techniques to reduce anxiety and get in the right zone before going into a meeting.**

Ask colleagues to give you feedback after a meeting on how you present, your posture and if you looked the person in the eye when you asked for a referral.

Chapter 6: Preparing to ask

Step 1: Homework

- **Has your client ever mentioned a contact that in your mind would make the perfect referral opportunity for you?**

Step 2: Find your bridge line

- **Ask for multifaceted feedback on the relationship.**
- **Describe how your business is going and explain you have now increased capacity.**
- **Describe the values and USPs of your firm that your client has experienced with you.**
- **Detail the history of the relationship: the initial aims of the relationship and how you have delivered.**
- **Use a schedule for the meeting to make your client aware you will bring up a referral request in the meeting.**
- **Leverage a strong friendship that has developed with your client.**

Chapter 7: Leading the conversation

Step 3: Ask for only one name

- **Ask for a referral to a person your client knows and has talked about.**
- **If a referral to this person is not possible, ask for ONE other person.**
- **Only ask for ONE name when asking for a referral. Listen to what you ask for in the next client meetings you have. Are you asking for ONE name only? If not, please try it and practise it. You will notice the difference it makes to success.**

Step 4: Qualify the referral

- **Be brave. Qualify precisely the sort of referral you are looking for to ensure you get the near perfect introduction. Try the next time to qualify precisely and listen to how it feels doing it this way. Notice how much clearer it is to ask the client for exactly what you want and the different sort of response your client gives.**

Step 5: Listening to the client's response

- **Listen intently to the client's response to your request. Who are they referring you to? If they cannot think of someone immediately, ask if you can get back to them in a week.**
- **If they said they could think of someone, did you ask them there and then who they were thinking of?**

Chapter 8: Step 6: Preparing your client

- Don't assume that the client will introduce you to the prospect in the best way to ensure that a referral meeting takes place.
- Manage this process directly to ensure your client knows the best language to use to approach the referral with their friend or colleague.

  This step is key to success and needs practice, as it will feel counter-intuitive to be trying to push or direct your client on HOW to ask their contact to meet you.
- One of the lines to use to initiate this: 'What has worked for me in the past is ... if you could ...'
- Ask permission to give the client a nudge if you have not heard anything from them in a week or 10 days.
- Do not ask for the phone number of the prospect before obtaining a referral from the client.
- Do not push for the client to set up an introductory meeting with all three of you. The most powerful method is a one-on-one meeting with the prospect.

Chapter 9: Step 7: Following up effectively

- About 30% of referrals don't happen because you failed to follow up your successful request to the client.
- You forget, you get too busy or become timid about reminding the client.
- Stay on top of your clients until they make the referral. They might forget or become too busy.
- If you do not get any response from the prospect, keep trying to call once every two weeks. Only send an email once.

Chapter 10: Asking for referrals from intermediaries

Challenge your existing intermediary strategy and make changes.

- Does the intermediary you are focused on to deliver a referral actually deliver referrals?
- Do they truly understand what you and your business do for clients?
- Do you really understand their business and client base to know how to help them?
- Are you helping them enough to find clients?
- Have you both discussed how best to receive a referral from each other?
- Be brave and very direct with your questions to your intermediaries to find out what you need to improve the relationship.
- Be honest and follow the matrix to see which intermediaries to focus on and which to drop.
- If you are at an early stage of your career without clients or with very few, be brave and show intermediaries a list of clients you want to approach to see if they can help.
- Organize a structured meeting with an intermediary to address all points of the matrix and move the relationship to a new level regarding referrals.
- Look at the existing list of intermediaries servicing your clients that you already have contact with. This is a super-powerful group for new referrals. In the wealth management, private client world this would be lawyers/ accountants/trustees of existing clients.

Chapter 11: Asking friends and family

- **Family and friends are a strong source of referrals.**
- **There will be mindsets that hold you back, but none must do so.**
  Don't take seriously thoughts such as:
  - **'They have known me since childhood.'**
  - **'They don't take me seriously in the workplace.'**
- **Make sure that you organize the meeting one-on-one in a business environment.**
- **Find ways to give back to this friend or family member so that you can reciprocate the help they are giving to you.**

Think as laterally as you can with friends and family – who might they be able to introduce you to?

Make a list of family and friends and put next to each name two people you would like to be introduced to, either a direct client prospect or a key intermediary.

Chapter 12: Making the most of internal referrals

- Your internal colleagues want to help you. You only need to ask.
- Help them in some way. Make it a reciprocal relationship.
- Expressing your thanks and gratitude for the help of this internal colleague is very important to ensure that they will help again.
- Treat internal colleagues like your best client and build the trust in the same way as with a client.
- If you succeed in getting a meeting with a referred prospect from a client, intermediary or an internal colleague and it becomes clear in your meeting that they will not become a client, ask that prospect for a referral anyway.
- Take advantage of cross-selling internal referrals. These internal referrals use strong existing client relationships to introduce your business' services or products to other divisions within the client's company.

Chapter 13: Using networking to ask for referrals

Networking at an event

- **Prepare before the event, finding out who is going and who you want to meet.**
- **Be ruthless about your time management. Focus on efficient prospecting before, at and following networking events.**
- **At the events, approach your prospects, keep it very short. Just get the meeting and then move off the subject.**
- **Use the line: 'Now is not the time. Let's put in a time to meet for a coffee/video call in the next couple of weeks.'**
- **Follow up immediately, strike while the iron is hot. Enthusiasm has a half-life, their enthusiasm to meet you will diminish by a half, each week.**

Before the next event/conference/dinner you are attending, ask yourself:

- *'How am I preparing differently for this event?'*
- *'How is my plan different? What am I doing that I have not done before?'*
- *'How am I approaching the follow-up to this event differently from before?'*

Using LinkedIn

- **Use LinkedIn to establish which of your contacts, personally known or not known by you, are NOW in an influential position where they might know one high-quality prospect.**
- **Use LinkedIn to establish which clients have a contact who could be a prospect.**
- **Do not write to these contacts asking them to make an introduction.**
- **Organize a coffee with your contact and then duplicate the advice given in previous chapters to achieve the referral.**
- **Prioritize your LinkedIn contacts, categorizing all your contacts into lists.**

1. Clients
2. Former clients
3. Current intermediaries
4. Family
5. Friends
6. Former work colleagues
7. Contacts you initiated via a mutual contact
8. Incoming contact requests.

Postscript: Asking in a pandemic

- Asking for a referral does not change due to the pandemic. You can ask all the clients and intermediaries.
- The only main change is that it is less easy to ask when the relationship is in an early stage.
- Becoming confident using video conferencing and utilizing this tool well while asking for a referral is important.
  Practise this and ask for feedback from your colleagues after meetings.
- Highlight the illustration of your firm's values and USPs during COVID-19.

Index